SUMMER RAMBLES

IN THE WEST.

BY

MRS. ELLET.

AUTHOR OF "PIONEER WOMEN OF THE WEST," ETC.

NEW-YORK:

J. C. RIKER, 129 FULTON-STREET.

M.DCCC.LIII.

JOHN F. TROW, PRINTER,
49 Ann-Street.

CONTENTS.

PAGE

XV.

SUMMER RAMBLES.

I.

DURING a visit at Sodus Bay, in June, 1852, an excursion was arranged, as far as Detroit and Milwaukie, to be extended farther if agreeable company should be found. Some weeks had been passed at the house of a relative on the banks of this lovely sheet of water, the scenery about which is not surpassed on the southern shore of Lake Ontario. The Bay, it may be remembered, lies midway between Oswego and the mouth of the Genesee River, a few hours' sail or drive from each. Its head is some twenty-five miles from the line of the Albany and Buffalo Railroad, and the direct railroad from Syracuse to Rochester passes much nearer. The "Sodus Point and Southern Railroad," about thirty-five miles in length, is now in progress; its design being to cross the new one between Rochester and Syracuse at the village of Newark, in Wayne County, and connect with the Canandaigua and Corning Railroad about nine miles north of Penn Yan, in Yates County. It is part of a great trunk line of railway from Lake Ontario to Washington City, intersecting at right angles the thoroughfares of nature and art which connect the valley of the Mississippi and the Lakes with the Atlantic cities, and running through the only natural opening in the great range of mountains separating the Atlantic from the Mississippi slope,—the valley of the Susquehanna. The Sodus Canal, connecting the Bay with the Erie Canal, is also in progress. The advantages afforded by these facilities of transportation, with the superiority of Sodus Bay as the finest harbor on the lake, surrounded by a fertile and populous farming country, cannot fail ere long to make it a prosperous place of business; while the beauty of its rural scenery will tempt many residents of our large cities to a summer sojourn in its vicinity. The lover of nature in her wildness and romance, however, will dread the transformation of those wooded headlands and islands into smooth fields and country-seats—inevitable as such a change must be in the progress of things.

It is said that a Scotch gentleman employed in the earliest survey of the country, after a ride through the deep forest, came suddenly in view of the boundless expanse of Ontario, and was so affected that he threw himself from his horse, and knelt in thankfulness that he had lived to behold so glorious a scene. The spot where this occurred, little changed by cultivation, may still awaken similar emotions. It is on the summit of a bluff overlooking the water; the smooth greensward is entirely free from underwood, but shaded by maples, beech and chestnut trees, hung with clusters of the wild grape-vine, which form the most beautiful natural arbors, wreathing the boughs in the utmost luxuriance, till they droop with their load of leaves. Behind is a charming dell, where a beechen grove is close enough to exclude the sun, while the winds from the lake have swept clean its grassy carpet. The banks break off in a perpendicular descent, and below, the blue waves are rippling and sparkling on the pebbly shore. Where the horizon joins the deep, repose piles of silver clouds edged with crimson, and the whole west, at sunset, is glowing with gold and purple, the rays spreading in many a brilliant streak across the bosom of the waters. The village is in sight: there is the school-house, with children playing on its green lawn, and many pretty cottages tastefully ornamented with the woodbine and honeysuckle, and white houses with gardens filled with fruit-trees and shrubbery.

Sodus Point—a small village, where still reside some of the early pioneers in this section of country—has become a favorite place of resort in summer, for the fishing and hunting afforded in the neighborhood, as well as its exquisite scenery. An Episcopal church is in process of building, and many new houses, for which there is an increasing demand. The place of worship has hitherto been at the village of Sodus, six miles distant, where there are several churches. The beautiful views afforded from the windows of any of the houses, cannot be impaired by cultivation. The lake is on the left, while the bay stretches far to the right, its sparkling waters, like a vast mirror set in a frame of deep green, encircled by its bold and wooded shores. Eastward, a lofty bluff rises above the lake, and along the banks of the bay, garlanding the whole Point, are groves of chestnut, tall, old and majestic, flinging their shadow on the calm waters at their feet. These groves were in former years places of meeting for rural pic-nic parties, and are still used for that purpose.

The 4th of July, 1852, was here celebrated by a rural fête; an oration was delivered in one of the groves, followed by a substantial repast, and a rustic dance, in a spacious arbor arranged for the occasion, with a fine display of fireworks in the evening, in front of the two hotels. The scene brought to mind many celebrations of the national festival in different spots on this shaded peninsula. One took place on a strip of land on the other side of the channel, where an old pioneer—a counterpart to Cooper's "Leatherstocking" —lived alone with his family, chiefly by hunting and fishing. Being fond of social gayety, he took upon himself, on this occasion, the office of entertainer. A calf and sheep were barbecued whole, after the primitive fashion, and huge pots of vegetables were set to boil over the fires kindled in the open air. The ladies of the company arranged the more delicate portions of the repast. The time till dinner was spent in what might be called a regular celebration of the day. The Declaration of Independence was read by one of the citizens; then the orator was called upon for a speech; and after that a rustic poet rose and rehearsed some indifferent verses in honor of his country. This done, the banquet, the portion of the celebration certainly most relished by all present, commenced. The wines drunk were of home manufacture, made of currants or gooseberries; yet they seemed to inspire as much wit and good humor as the most costly imported ones. After dinner, the different parties dispersed; some to walk on the clean, pebbly beach; some to go on sailing excursions, or watch the fishermen; while here and there might be seen groups seated in the groves, passing the hours away with jest, and story, and song, till the lengthening shadows warned them that their day of festivity was closed.

At another celebration of this anniversary, a singular incident occurred. Several parties engaged a schooner for a short excursion upon the lake, and as the day was calm and bright, it was not thought necessary to employ any other seamen than the two lads who had charge of her in cruising up and down the bay. The different groups on board were merry enough, and cheerily bade farewell to their friends upon the pier, who watched their bark as she moved like a white-winged bird over the waters, her masts gay with pennons, and her deck crowded. There was one, however, insensible to mirth. He was insane: but his madness being of a gentle and melancholy cast, he was suffered to go wherever he pleased. He was fond of mingling in scenes of this kind, though his pale, sad face, and wasted figure might, if they had been noticed at all, have thrown a gloom over the gayety of the company. He sat at one end of the deck, wrapped in his cloak, though the day was warm, never smiling at any of the jests uttered in his hearing, but apparently enjoying, as much as he could enjoy, the fresh air, and their swift motion through the water. He had once, himself, been in command of a vessel, and loved nothing so well as a "rover's life."

They had been out scarcely an hour, when they were overtaken by one of those sudden tempests so common on our great lakes. Clouds began to swell upward from the edge of the horizon, rent by angry streaks of lightning; and the wind increased to such a degree, that the waves occasionally broke over the deck of the vessel. As it often happens, the party on board did not become sensible of their danger till the storm was upon them. It grew more violent; and to add to their alarm, it soon became evident that the imperfect skill and strength of the young seamen were quite insufficient to manage the vessel. Without careful management, they could not hope to make the harbor, but must inevitably be driven further out, and beyond the reach of help, should help be required. The confusion became general. At this moment, the crazy captain, who had sat motionless for a long while, suddenly rose to his feet, walked across the deck, and in a commanding voice, began to give directions for the management of the vessel. His orders were instantly obeyed. All knew his skill and experience as a sailor, and none doubted that in this hour of danger his aid was invaluable. He threw off his cloak, and went vigorously to work; measured the wild waters with a calm and practised eye, and soon set all right. In a few moments the vessel glided safely between the narrow piers, and as she sailed over the smooth sheet within, her passengers found time to thank the poor maniac, whose timely exertions had been of such use to them.

One of the prominent headlands seen in sailing up the bay, was many years since improved by a community of Shakers, a branch of the Society at Lebanon. They disposed of their land and buildings, and removed elsewhere. But the hill, crowned with their little settlement, has a cheerful aspect, and contrasts with the wild and solitary appearance of another headland to the west, covered with dark green woods to the water's edge. There are three islands of considerable size in this bay. The largest is partially cultivated, and is a beautiful site for a country residence. The others are richly wooded to the water, and their bold shores are only approached by fishermen, when they draw their nets laden with the delicious treasures. The water is so clear, you can see the shells and stones on the bottom at a great depth, and watch the unconscious fish sporting about the tempting hook. As far as our eye can reach, the bay is dotted with fishing-boats, and some are drawing their nets on a little sandy shoal, scarce broad enough to enable them to moor their boat. Now a fresh breeze springs up, and the swell increases. The sport is over for the present. The small boats retreat behind the islands, where they are sheltered from the northwest winds.

In winter, this noble sheet presents a beautiful

spectacle. The ice is several feet in thickness, and abundantly strong enough to bear a sleigh and pair of horses. Its surface is clear as glass, and is an admirable field for skaters, who cross each other's path like spirits, wearing, however, very unghostly apparel: to wit, coarse overcoats, caps and mittens. Not long since an *ice-boat* was constructed here, water-tight, made to go on runners like an ordinary sleigh, and furnished with ample sails. By proper management, a vehicle of this kind might be made to sail in almost any direction, propelled by the wind.

Here, also, in dearth of winter amusements, a *whirligig* is sometimes set up on the ice. A post is firmly fixed in the centre, and a wheel, made to revolve by horse-power, whirls about a small sled, fastened to it by a rope. The sled describes a circle proportioned to the length of the rope, and flies with immense velocity. This was at one time a favorite amusement, though an extremely dangerous one. Not only is there danger that the rope will break, and send the vehicle no one knows whither, but the ice in some spots may be thin. The "channel," a broad line through the midst of the bay, seldom freezes so as to be crossed safely, and is always carefully avoided by those who pass from one shore to the other.

At the head of navigation, a bridge crosses the bay, and here is a magnificent view. The eye can now measure the extent of the bay. Its smooth expanse is bounded on either side by an irregular line of bold shore, covered with thick woods; its islands rise abruptly and majestically from the deep, and it is impossible to imagine the fine effect of those hills of dense foliage, in contrast to the fair blue of the waters on which they rest, and on which peacefully sleep their broad shadows. The wide, calm sheet of water, whether ruddy with the last rays of the sun, or lightly rippled by the breeze, is a sight of indescribable beauty. In the remote distance is the fringed line of white sand that incloses the bay, and beyond, the boundless lake.

The woods along the shore afford some beautiful rides and drives. Sometimes young and slender trees on either side of the path meet overhead, and form a canopy excluding the sun; festoons of wild grape-vines hanging thickly over the boughs. The cultivated country, sloping on every side to the water, is rich with the most luxuriant vegetation; pasture lands of fresh green are varied by fields waving with the yellow harvest. Neat looking farm-houses are scattered in every direction; and some pretty, ornamental cottages, fronted by groves of chestnut and other young trees, may be seen close to the water. A little cultivation would convert the woodlands into a fertile, smiling country, and rich harvests would well reward the farmer's toil.

On the eastern shore in a sheltered situation, is a stately grove of elms, shading a spot consecrated to affection and sorrow. It is a family burial ground; the inscriptions on the monuments tell us that a young mother and three lovely children repose here. They sleep not more peacefully, thus lulled by the murmur of waters and the rustling of foliage, than in burial places less secluded and romantic; but the solemn beauty of their resting-place is pleasant to friends who visit the sacred spot.

But it was on a joyous occasion that our westward tour was discussed. Dr. C——'s beautiful country-seat, three miles north of Sodus, is the admiration of every passer by, for the tasteful disposition of its grounds, the picturesque views it affords, its ornamental flower-gardens and neat mansion. It is surrounded by a plantation of young locust trees, and a thick grove of these, on one side, is almost impervious to the sun at noonday. A winding avenue, shaded with trees, leads from the gate to the door, where the visitor ever meets that hospitable and cheerful welcome, which enlivens like the sunshine. From the verandah, the pillars of which are wreathed with flowering vines, the blue line of Lake Ontario appears through the distant woods, and the intervening space is filled up with clusters of forest trees, smooth fields waving with grain, and an orchard rich with the promise of golden stores. On this occasion a large party of guests from different directions within four or five miles, was assembled for a rural tea-drinking. They had come at an early hour in the afternoon, according to country custom, and were walking over the grounds, admiring the rare flowers which had been the special care of Mrs. C—— and her sister, or inhaling the cool and fragrant breeze at the drawing-room windows opening on the piazza, listening to music that might have graced a city concert room. There was no lack of lions, chief among whom was the pastor of the parish, endowed by nature with extraordinary musical talent, which had been highly cultivated, and with a voice whose full and rich melody might be envied by a professed artist. He was master of several instruments, it was said, and had taken much pains to improve the sacred music in his church, somewhat to the discontent of concert-hating gossips, who thought "the nasal twang heard at conventicle" in old times, better than modern innovations. There was also a lady practitioner of medicine from a neighboring village, in advance of the recent movements, for she had been a professor of the healing art nearly twenty years. Her studies were prosecuted with her husband, a physician of established repute, and under his auspices she commenced practice, having her own set of patients, the number of which soon increased rapidly. Both continued to ride their respective rounds in attendance on the sick, the lady employed chiefly by the suffering of her own sex and for children, and possessing the entire confidence of all her acquaintance. It may be supposed that consultations were held in difficult cases.

Since our meeting on that occasion, Dr. G. has been called from this world. His many virtues and sincere piety had endeared him to a large circle of friends, and the whole community mourn his loss. Mrs. G. is a woman of admirable energy, and has reared a large family of children, attending to the concerns of her household, as well as her professional duties. Those interested in the establishment of a medical college for women, should publish reports of the cases treated successfully in her practice.

In our company were also several descendants of a heroine of the Revolution, whose eventful history has been elsewhere recorded. When the hour came for parting with our friends, it was amusing to see the impatience of the horses attached to the several carriages, whose compelled stand-still for so many hours had been something of a contrast to the social enjoyment of their owners. They pranced, and snorted, and started, and there was not a little fright and confusion, as one party after another took their places, and were whirled away with unaccustomed rapidity down the road. It was a sweet moonlight evening, and fresh with the breath of young summer; and long will that pleasant re-union be remembered by those who had part in it.

On the third of July—the fourth falling on Sunday—there was a boat race from the bridge near the head of the bay, some miles down. The day was bright, but the northwest wind, which often blows fiercely from the lake, was very high, and lifted the waters in foam-crested waves that threatened destruction to the small but gallant crafts which, with all their sails set, were beating resolutely against the driving gale. From the chestnut grove in front of my brother's residence, an elevation overlooking the bay, it was interesting to see the boats cross swiftly from one side to the other, each strained to its utmost speed to distance competitors and obtain the prize, its sails almost dipping into the blue waters, and the sailors displaying their skill in the sudden turns made on every tack. Many guesses were hazarded at first as to which would be successful, but the question was soon set at rest, as one slender vessel shot ahead, and continued to maintain its superiority. On the fifth our family party dined at Wood's hotel, at the Point, occupying a division of the table where some eighty country folk were seated to make merry on the good cheer, consisting of roast pig, goose, and mutton, puddings, tarts, and fruits of the season, without wines or any beverage stronger than lemonade. Such is the regular routine of Independence dinners in the country, and may it be long before our stout farmers introduce in their social gatherings the deleterious drinks esteemed indispensable to metropolitan hilarity!

Our departure for the West had been appointed the following day, and as our circle did not expect in months to meet again, the afternoon and evening were passed quietly. Little Willie and Max were every where, taking part in the busy scenes around them with the earnest delight of boyhood, and our beautiful Florence, with her sweet fairy laugh, echoed all the mirth she saw, joined heartily by her cherub brother Charlie, three years old, opening his large dark eyes in wonder at so many strangers. It was late in the evening when the fireworks were ended, and having invoked many blessings on the dear children, and bidden adieu to numerous friends, the travellers returned to the hospitable mansion of Mr. F., making preparations to set off at four o'clock the next morning.

II.

VERY early in the morning we took our places—three ladies, and a young gentleman who was to be our escort—in a large covered carriage, our luggage following in a wagon, and commenced the journey to Rochester. The road kept the lake in sight for about three miles, and many a picturesque view was afforded as we emerged from some shadowy dell, or a portion of the primeval forest, of the limitless expanse of blue waters sparkling with the earliest sunbeams. At Sodus we took the "Ridge Road," which runs along a continuous ridge three or four miles from the lake, supposed to have been in former ages the boundary of the waters. Here we were joined by Mrs. R., who with her son was to be our companion to Detroit, her husband and Mr. F. accompanying us as far as Rochester. As the day advanced, the heat was intense, and the dust from roads that had not known showers in many days, almost suffocating. We stopped for an hour's rest at Williamson's Corners, and were cordially invited by the landlady to partake of lunch from a table loaded with the remains of Independence cheer; fragments of roast pig, huge hams dressed with cut paper, segments of chicken pie and other delicacies, claimed our attention, but a glass of cool lemonade was much more acceptable. We resumed our journey, and after skirting the picturesque marshy bay which reaches up several miles from the lake between a range of wooded hills, entered the city of Rochester a little after two, just too late for the expected train. We did not so much regret the delay, as it afforded time for removing the dust of our drive, and a walk about the city. A large hotel near the dépôt of the railroad was our stopping place for three hours, and afforded an excellent dinner. After a suitable rest some of the party set off on a shopping excursion, but had scarcely crossed the street when the shrill whistle of the engine and rush of the cars announced the arrival of the eastern express train; and forgetful that three quarters of an hour were lacking of their starting time, our inexperienced travellers made all haste to check the baggage and secure seats. The large dépôt was hung with black drapery, and crowded with people wearing badges of mourning; for the body of Henry Clay was to be brought in the "lightning train" from New-York that day, on the way to Lexington, Kentucky; and the mistake of supposing it aboard the evening express car was very general. At every station along the road we found funeral processions, with solemn music and the booming of cannon, and other signs of mourning, the same impression seeming to prevail, that our train bore the remains of the illustrious statesman, and the people coming from every direction to pay the last token of their respect. The crowd at

Buffalo was immense, and it was with some difficulty, having an inexperienced guide, that we threaded our way to the omnibus which was to convey us to the steamboat. Such a confusion of tongues, and clamor of porters, and hurrying to and fro of passengers, each intent on his own business or pleasure, and jostling regardlessly against his neighbor! The increasing darkness, and vehement altercation of the agents of rival lines for passengers, with the thousand and one directions bawled out in every variety of tone and temper, and the rumbling and rushing of vehicles and feet quite bewildered us, and with a confused notion of being carried in the whirl we knew not whither, we could hardly be persuaded even to trust the representations of the honest driver destined for the May Flower.

The night was still and beautifully clear, and its romantic repose contrasted strangely with the wild and thronged aspect of the shores and decks of the several boats bound up the lake. The busy tread of men passing and repassing, the rolling of barrows, the shouting and calling, and rapid conversation, the crowds pressing on board, and over all the streaming light of the lamps, formed a scene we were glad to escape by retiring as soon as possible to the magnificent saloon of the steamboat. The traveller who has a ticket on this line, the Michigan Central, need give himself no trouble about his luggage. The elegance and luxurious comfort of these boats are unsurpassed, with their spacious and richly furnished state-rooms, sumptuous tables, and ample provision for the accommodation of large numbers, and the most considerate attention is given to provide for every possible want. One meets with more of this gratifying sort of attention at the West than elsewhere, and I have been struck with the intelligence of some of the servants. A lady somewhat noted as a writer was not long since complimented by a colored stewardess, who came to her state-room to pay her respects to one whose works she had read. On being asked how she knew her, she replied that she had recognized her by a portrait recently published. A curious fancy is that of naming the choice state-rooms after authoresses of distinction, and it sounds rather comical to hear that "somebody in Mrs. Barbauld is sick," or "a gentleman wishes to speak with a lady at the door of Hannah More," or "some ice is wanted in Mrs. Hemans." Several living female writers of celebrity are thus distinguished on board the May Flower. The apartment occupied by Jenny Lind is still adorned with its regal decorations, and was appropriated by a newly wedded pair.

The starting of the boats from Buffalo was delayed till near midnight, their usual hour being nine in the evening. The stars were reflected in the bosom of Erie, which was scarcely ruffled by the light breeze as we swept onward in our floating palace. We had no rough weather or sea-sickness to mar enjoyment of the trip, and the passengers appeared pleased with themselves and every thing about them. If they were not, it was no fault of the officers or the arrangements. We now began to feel ourselves once more within the bounds of the Great West, where the very air is bracing with the spirit of freedom and enterprise. We entered Detroit River without much thought of the historical associations connected with it, and saw the sunshine dancing merrily on its green waters, as we approached the city of the straits, with a feeling of pleasure that we had been safely brought over a perilous part of our journey, and were soon to be greeted by smiles of welcome from loving friends. We landed at Detroit about four o'clock in the afternoon, in time for passengers to take the evening train to Chicago, where they would arrive early on the following morning.

Three of our party proceeded to our friend's house, and were welcomed in a charming family circle. We had time to talk over the chances and changes of the year that had rolled away since we last met. One engagement had taken place, and a lovely young girl who shared the perils and delights of our voyage up Lakes St. Clair, Huron, and Superior, and enslaved a score of hearts, having at last surrendered her own, was soon to wear the bridal veil. No wonder that the days passed rapidly, and the 20th of July came, before we were actually upon the journey so long anticipated. It was four o'clock in the afternoon when, accompanied by several friends, we drove to the spacious dépôt of the Michigan Central Railroad. The completion of this extensive and beautiful road opened new prospects for the whole State, and an expeditious and easy communication between the Atlantic country and the northwest. It saves the perilous voyage up the great Lakes, and when the communication to Galena is complete, will make it a "quick step" to the Mississippi. The morning train for Chicago left Detroit at nine o'clock; the evening at five. It is worthy of notice that both in leaving and returning, the dépôt is kept clear of the clamorous crowd of hackmen, porters, and "runners," who usually confuse the traveller at a stopping-place, so that ample room and leisure are afforded to have every thing done in order. The same propriety is observed on the entire route from Buffalo westward.

The country is level for many miles after leaving Detroit; only redeemed by the slightest possible undulation from the flatness of prairie-land, yet fertile with rich fields of ripening grain, patches of meadow, and tracts of heavily timbered land. Occasionally new "clearings" remind one of olden times, and the log houses are generally very neat in their appearance. There is a peculiar beauty in these woods: the trees are lofty, and have more spreading tops than is usual in the primeval forest. Extensive groves, or rather orchards, of the "weeping elm," with its luxuriant trailing foliage, the straight, tall trunks entwined with the wild creeper, give a picturesque loveliness to the landscape. Their drapery, though of brilliant green, brings to mind the stately southern swamp trees, covered with the moss that waves like a shroud among their leaves. Here and there clusters of young oaks, looking like a nursery of fruit trees, and thickets of bushes fringing some winding stream, vary the forest scenery. Passing two pretty villages, we find the country more varied and broken as we approach Ypsilanti, a thriving little town, with broad streets well shaded by old forest trees, and many country seats tastefully adorned with gardens and groves. The winding Huron, flowing gently along to mingle its clear waters with Lake Erie, is as serpentine as the Housatonic. The track crosses it seven times within a few miles. It is the pride of Washtenaw county, and has been called, by a resident poet, "the bright, swift river of the bark canoe;" but its day of romance is over, now that the cars, with their freight of busy energies, rush past its waters twice every day. Bordered by thick bushes, bending willows, or oaks, or bursting from the close embrace of the woods like a nymph from her leafy bower, it gives us glimpses of enchanting scenery, and presently the eye is caught by one of the peculiar features of a Michigan landscape, the oak openings. The dense forest, with its luxuriant garniture, is varied here and there by park-like slopes, thinly sprinkled with ancient oaks, shading a greensward enamelled with wild flowers, or partially covered with an undergrowth of dwarf bushes. Occasionally, groups stand at intervals in the open space, and groves of young trees, most gracefully disposed in the picture, rival the art of the landscape gardener. The uplands swell gradually into hills, which are of imposing height around Ann Arbor, all adorned with these beautiful openings. A winding dell, stretching a mile or two from the village, affords the most charming of walks under the shade of oaks and elms that sturdily maintain their right of soil: it is called "Glen Mary"

—and I believe had a title to the name before the one which has been made classic by a poet's reveries.

The village of Ann Arbor has now nearly four thousand inhabitants, several churches of different denominations, a flourishing Female Seminary under the care of the Misses Clark, and a University maintained by the State. The first settlers came about 1824, and lodged for some weeks under the shelter of their sleigh-box and a rude bower of trees covered with buffalo-skins. This primitive arbor, or the beauty of the oak groves, furnished a name to the place, and the prefix "Ann," was given in honor of the name of the wives of two of the pioneers. The first garden was on the spot now occupied by the public square, and formerly a place of council for the Indians. The village, with its surroundings of fine natural scenery, is often visited by travellers, and is important as the site of the first established literary institution of Michigan. The buildings, half a mile from the town, are neat and spacious, and advantageously situated; the ground commanding superb views on every side. The library is not large, but is well selected. A fine building, a few rods across the green, is appropriated to the Medical department, and four handsome houses at the corners, with large gardens, are occupied by the Professors.

We spent the evening with a most agreeable family in Ann Arbor, two of the members of which were to be of our travelling party. Several of the kind neighbors came in, with friendly counsel and good wishes, and well laden with these, we stood on the morrow a little before eleven, at the dépôt, awaiting the rapidly approaching cars. The day was excessively warm, and a prolonged drought rendered dust inevitable, though the large and commodious cars, clean and luxuriously furnished, and not too crowded, offered all the comfort that could be had under the circumstances. Nor should we forget to notice the care for the traveller's refreshment so quietly manifested in the provision of pails of iced water, both on the cars and at the stations, invitingly arranged with dippers at hand, and calling forth mental expressions of gratitude in such weather.

The rapid view obtained of the interior of Michigan, while one is whirled along at the rate of twenty-five miles an hour over the great central road which traverses the peninsula, gives one an agreeable idea of the country. Its general features are soft and pleasing, without strikingly picturesque scenery; bespeaking fertility of soil and careful cultivation, with the prosperity attendant on such circumstances. The villages have a clean and thriving aspect; and the winding streams that now and then coquettishly break upon the sight, crossed by the iron track and disappearing in the embrace of the woods, with the clear lakelets bordered by strips of marshland or clustering foliage, are most refreshing to the eye. The Huron thus lingers for many miles, as if unwilling to be lost to the traveller's view. Everywhere the beautiful wild oaklands border the road, and stretch onward for miles. Sometimes these groves are so close and umbrageous as almost to have the character of woods; again, they are stately parks of ancient looking trees, with broad patches of sunshine lying between their shadows on the waving, wild grass. There are many thick nurseries of young oaks growing up to form these majestic orchards in time, if not removed by the hand of "improvement," which has already made devastation in the beauty of the undulating landscape.

Leoni is a township had in remembrance as the place where many of the conspirators involved in the late trial for a conspiracy to injure the railroad, lived; and the mischief was said to have originated hereabouts. One of the accused was an early emigrant to Michigan, by the name of Filley, whose misfortunes excited sympathy and interest in all who heard his story. The circumstances resemble those of the capture of Frances Slocum at Wyoming, familiar to readers of our border history, and are worth relating as illustrative of the dangers to which pioneer residents were exposed.

Ami Filley was a native of Windsor, Connecticut, and in 1831 married a daughter of Colonel William Marvin, of Granville, in Massachusetts. Three or four years after, he removed with his family to the locality afterwards occupied by the town of Jackson, in Michigan. It was then a wilderness. He settled here, and by industry and good management soon found himself in possession of a productive farm, while by the rapid incoming of emigrants, the place grew into a populous and flourishing village. Numerous tribes of Indians were in the vicinity, and whole wandering families often visited the homes of the white people, yet an amicable understanding always prevailed between them, and nothing had occurred to disturb these friendly relations.

In August of the year 1837, Filley's little son, a child five years of age, was taken by Mary Mount, the hired girl, into a swamp a mile or so distant, to gather whortleberries. The father at that time was in the field harvesting: the swamp was not far from the residence of the girl's father, and one account states that Mary was joined by her sister. The boy, it seems, became tired or sleepy, and wanted to go home; and about four o'clock Mary took him to the road and told him to run on to Mount's house, which was in sight, and wait for her. When she had picked her supply of berries, she went to her father's, but learned that little William had not been there. Supposing that the child had gone home, she proceeded to Mr. Filley's, but found he had not returned. The alarmed parents instantly set out to search for him, and were assisted by the neighbors, for the news soon spread through the village and its vicinity; watchfires were kept up all night, and though in the midst of harvest, all labor was suspended, in the anxiety every one felt for the recovery of the child. For more than a week the search was kept up, day and night, and every rod of ground, every nook and thicket, were thoroughly examined for more than thirty miles around. Every pond and stream was dragged, and as an encouragement to continue the search, Filley offered a reward for the recovery even of the body of his child, in the papers printed in different parts of the country. Some had suspicions of foul play, and a careful search was made, not only in the swamp, but on Mount's premises; even the floor of his cellar was taken up; but nothing was found to justify proceedings against the girl. One circumstance pointed conjecture in a different direction. Two miles from the swamp, on an Indian trail, a paper with a picture was found, which it was remembered the little fellow had as a plaything when he was last seen. When asked if he had ever any difficulty with the Indians, which might have caused feelings of animosity towards him, Filley called to mind that he had once struck one of them, who had been in the habit of coming with his companions and helping himself at his house to what he liked. Filley had remonstrated against this intrusion and robbery several times, and when he enforced his reproof with blows, the savages departed with threats of vengeance. The little boy had always been fond of them, and it might be that they had retaliated by stealing him. Another cause of resentment is said to have been Filley's having ploughed up an old Indian burial-ground.

Inquiries were made among the different tribes and families in the vicinity, and large offers of reward tendered to the chiefs and leading men, but no satisfactory result followed. Mr. Filley left his home and traversed the wilds of Michigan, Wisconsin, and Iowa, in the hope of gaining some intelligence, but all his efforts were vain, and he returned to the heartbroken mother with the sad certainty that their little William was lost!

For several years the stricken family endured this worse affliction than the bereavement of death; for had they buried their child, time would have softened grief, and the certainty that his pure spirit had taken its departure to a world of happiness, would have been a deep consolation. But the awful uncertainty that hung over his fate, and the reflection that he might have fallen into cruel hands, or be brought up amidst scenes of violence and bloodshed, caused an abiding sorrow. As time rolled on, hope was extinguished, but the lost one was not forgotten, and every hour of peace was darkened by the harrowing thoughts and fears associated with their calamity. The mother became the prey of a lingering disease, and at length sank into the grave.

Some time after Mrs. Filley's death, letters were received from Filley's former residence in Connecticut, in which mention was made of a boy taken from some wandering Indians in Albany, supposed to be the same who had been stolen in Michigan. The authorities of the city hearing that a white child was with the savages, caused the arrest of those who claimed him, and endeavored to compel them to confess whence he had been brought. The Indians, however, obstinately refused to make any disclosure, though alternately coaxed and threatened, and were finally dismissed, the boy being placed in the Orphan Asylum. In 1844, a Mr. Cowles, of Tolland, Massachusetts, happening to be in Albany, heard of this boy as one suitable to have bound to him as a servant, applied for him and took him home. His history was told as an interesting one, and not long after, the Rev. Dr. Cooley, of Granville, who visited the place and heard the story, came to the conclusion that it was no other than Filley's son. He had heard the details of the loss from the boy's grandfather, Col. Marvin, near whom he had lived. He immediately communicated to Marvin the information obtained, and no time was lost by the latter in sending the tidings to Filley, who happened then to be on a visit to his old home in Connecticut. He went at once to Tolland, where the lad still remained, and from an account that was circulated in Jackson the following year, it seemed that he was firmly convinced, by the appearance of the boy, that he was no other than his own. The boy had a distinct recollection of having been sent to school among white children; he also recollected that at his old home there were two babies, who were always kept in a box together; this was really the case, as Mrs. Filley had twins. After his capture, he had constantly resided in the same family, which consisted of four Indians—Paul and Phebe Ann Prye, Martha their daughter, and a man who lived with them. They adopted the white child as their son, and he was taught to believe that he was really so; in fact, he supposed himself an Indian boy, and was not aware of any difference of complexion or blood till he was taken away from his companions at Albany. The first place he remembered visiting was Green Bay, of the scenery of which he gave a tolerably correct description. In travelling thither the Indians either went or returned by water, as he remembered being on board a steamboat. In their wanderings he would sometimes be sent to beg clothes or food for himself and the family. During the summers they made peregrinations through Michigan and New-York, occasionally visiting Connecticut, and at one time were encamped at Stonington for several weeks. In the winters they quartered themselves in wigwams, in the neighborhood of some village, subsisting on rabbits and other small game, and feasting sometimes on bullfrogs. They manufactured baskets, with which they often sent the boy to the nearest grocery to buy whiskey. He remembered particularly living near Detroit, Utica, Brothertown, Catskill, and Hudson, and being several months at Hillsdale, in New-York. Both in summer and winter, in all their wanderings, he travelled barefoot, suffering often from cold, hunger, and fatigue; but the kindness of his Indian sister, who was very much attached to him, made his life cheerful.

The circumstances of the case rendered it highly probable that this was the lost boy; age and appearance corresponded, and the father's first conviction was that he indeed embraced his son; but doubts afterwards arose as to his identity. Filley returned to Michigan without the boy, to the astonishment and chagrin of his friends; and in time circumstances came to light which tended to show that this lad was the son of an Indian woman, by a man of wealth and high political standing, in Columbia county, New-York, who had threatened the mother with punishment if she revealed the child's paternity.

The mystery that enveloped this case has never been cleared up. Filley does not believe the boy his own, though many of his neighbors and friends are inclined to think otherwise, and suppose him influenced by the stepmother's unwillingness to receive the young stranger. His relatives, on the other hand, cling to the belief that it is the lost William, and the boy is now residing with Filley's sister, in Windsor, Connecticut.

Jackson, situated on a stream called Grand River, is a place of considerable business, and has the State Prison, a large and long building, which shows to advantage about half a mile from the road. At Albion the Female Seminary, a Wesleyan Institution, stands on an elevation commanding a fine view. The buildings are spacious and neat, and surrounded by extensive grounds.

The heat became intense as the day advanced, the dust seemed to thicken, and the stoppage at Marshall for dinner was hailed with pleasure as affording a few moments for at least partial ablutions. By the time these were made, the passengers who filled up the long table had nearly finished their repast; a venture among them was not to be thought of by timid women, besides that the ominous whistle gave notice that the train was in readiness to start; so we were forced to be content with a square bit of cheese and a few crackers purchased in haste from the clerk, who reproached us for having wasted so much time in needless preparatories,—needless in sooth, so far as the preservation of neatness was concerned, for we could not "stay dusted" five minutes. Here we had the first sight of the pretty stream called the Kalamazoo River. The oak groves all along are enamelled with wild flowers, the loveliness of which might escape the eye of the ordinary traveller, but will reward attentive observation. M—— counted forty-five varieties on the way, the botanic names of which she duly noted down; she is an enthusiast in the science, and will find enough to delight her in our north-western trip.

Not far from Galesburg is the deserted institution of "Alphadelphia," established by some disciples of Fourier a few years since. After leaving Niles, the hills become more prominent and the country more broken, and occasionally covered with patches of heavy timber. Some of the log cabins were rude enough to remind us of pioneer days, and built in that primitive style—the logs projecting at the corners. After an hour's travel, the whistle announced that we were near New Buffalo, and the boundless expanse of Lake Michigan, all ablaze with the beams of the westering sun, burst on the sight. The track takes a southward turn, and shortly after crosses the line of Indiana, keeping the lake in view for some time, till its blue waters vanish behind masses of dense foliage. Before long we come upon tracts of prairie land, extending from the head of the lake. Here and there a cabin or shanty, rudely constructed, is the home of laborers who have found employment on the road. The women at work, and the men smoking or mending fishing-tackle out of doors, afford a picture of emigrant life hardly suited to the advancement of a railway; here it is simply homely, while it would be poetical a few degrees further north and west. The scene of the Chicago massacre in 1812, is hereabouts.* The sunset glow was yet lingering in the west as the train stopped, about a mile out of the city of Chicago. The handsome dépôt not being finished, the passengers arriving were at the mercy of rival hackmen, of whom, in other stopping-places on the route, the way was kept pleasantly clear.

* See PIONEER WOMEN OF THE WEST,—Memoir of Mrs. Heald.

III.

THE sky darkened while Mr. C. was waiting to get our luggage together, amidst a scene of confusion and clamor, and we were glad to find ourselves gathered into the carriage belonging to the Hamilton House. Two of the party were first to be driven to the house of Judge W. We knew not an inch of the way, and the driver proved as ignorant as ourselves, for he carried us in every direction about the city in search of the new residence of the family, who had removed from their old one a few days previous. We stopped in front of a score of houses with lawns and "a new gate-post," but at last lighted upon the mansion, pleasantly situated on Michigan avenue. It was past ten o'clock, however, and the lower rooms were ominously dark, while a faint glimmer in one of the upper windows showed that the last sitter up had retired. A stout knock or two caused the movement of the light, and presently Mr. and Miss C. were received within, while we only waited the removal of the luggage. But the kind gentleman of the mansion came out the next moment, and insisted that Miss S. and myself should share his hospitality. In vain were our reiterated refusals; in vain our representations of the sad condition to which the day's travel had reduced us; in vain our promises to come on the morrow; persevering kindness overruled all objections. We were led into the house with injunctions to be careful about stepping among the boards and fresh plaster mixed for use, and immediately supplied with the abundance of cool water required as the first thing necessary to comfort. I must not forget to notice that the proprietor of the Hamilton House, with Western courtesy, refused to depart from his rule of transporting passengers without charge, though we did not become his guests.

There are many degrees of welcome, and many different ways of expressing it, more grateful to the heart than any demonstration through the medium of customary phrases. Miss Sedgwick somewhere says her ideal is realized, when the new comer is received with an unclouded brow in a house so crowded that the young lady has to sleep on a lounge in her room, where she tells her beloved guest the news of the family. Brighter still is the token, when the friends of the guest, and her friends' friends, are for her sake received to home and heart, though the unfinished house be still in the hands of masons and carpenters; when the sweet lady of the mansion and her charming daughter prepare with their own hands (the servants having retired) the late meal for the refreshment of weary and dusty wanderers, who are somewhat doubtful if less than "all great Neptune's ocean" will suffice for a thorough cleansing; when no scheme of going to a hotel will be listened to, and strangers are made to feel at home by such heartfelt genialities of

2*

kindness as only heart-proceeding courtesy could devise. The kindness was the more cheering, as one of the ladies in our party suffered all next day from illness which required the quiet and care of a home for her restoration.

A pleasant drive on the following morning showed us Chicago in its best and busiest aspect. The streets are broad and not too compactly built up, and the city generally is spacious and open, and has an airy appearance —albeit the plank streets in its business part are far from clean. The Chicago River winds its serpentine course through the midst, and vessels sail on its bosom, the bridges opening to let them pass through, and closing immediately for the passage of carriages. The most desirable and fashionable residences are on Michigan avenue, between which and the lake is an inclosed strip of public land, set out with trees; it will form in time one of the most magnificent drives in any city on the continent. The prairies extend on all sides, far as the eye can reach, level as the blue expanse they border, and sending over the thronged city the breezes sweeping across their boundless wastes. Many of the better class of houses have pretty gardens, and a space for shrubbery in front, and in the principal avenues there is room for the planting of trees by each proprietor between the side-walk and the street. One of the curiosities of the place is the Presbyterian church, semi-gothic in architecture, and built of a variegated blue and black limestone brought from the prairies. The marine hospital is built of cream-colored Chicago brick. The principal hotels are in the heart of the town, and built substantially, without pretension to ornament. The city is growing fast, and has already a population of nearly fifty thousand. It is called "the Garden City," probably on account of the numerous gardens in its vicinity, from which fine views may be had of the surrounding country. One of these, belonging to Dr. Egan, our friends took us to see in the afternoon, and its intelligent proprietor pointed out the different localities. The city limits extend so far out as to afford room for a vast increase of population; a few years, however, may see them filled up. Great numbers of cattle may be seen feeding on the prairies, and we were informed that it is customary for those residents who keep cows, to give them every morning into the charge of a herdsman, who takes them out, tends them while they feed all day, and brings them home at night. Far as the eye can reach, a slightly elevated ridge may be seen, on which part the streams whose waters are to flow into the St. Lawrence, or find their rest in the Gulf of Mexico; and so near are the sources of each, that at the breaking up of winter an accident may lead either way the contribution of a chance rivulet.

The society of Chicago must be excellent, if one can be allowed to judge from the very agreeable specimens we saw in our day's sojourn. Mrs. K., one of our new acquaintances, is the daughter-in-law of the earliest resident of the place, whose trading establishment stood near the junction of the river with the lake, when the peninsula of Michigan was a wilderness, peopled only with savages, and but one or two settlers, besides the men of the garrison, lived here. Many members of Mr. K.'s family were associated with the early history of this region of country, and a sister-in-law was preserved from massacre in the famous battle with the Indians, by a friendly chief, who dragged her out in the lake and held her in the water until she could be led off in safety. Mrs. K. herself described several excursions on horseback through the primeval forests of Illinois, before the pioneer settlers had yet penetrated its northern portions, and her camping out, or lodging with no roof save the canopy of heaven.

A splendid panoramic view of the city and surrounding country can be had from an observatory on the top of the Tremont House. On this picture our eyes rested while the purple of sunset faded from the west, and the young moon rode through the clear ether, and the blue lake lay in shadow, while myriad lamps, lighting up as by magic, far and wide, showed us the peopled city still alive with activity, labor, and care, which the dark and solemn night cannot put to rest.

The evening passed in a charming circle of visitors, and after an early breakfast on the 23d, we bade farewell to our kind friends and drove to the cars of the "Galena and Chicago Union Railroad," which started at half past seven. Happy may the traveller conclude himself when the completion of the road may enable him to have the prospect, even with slow travel, of reaching Galena the same evening. A new route will then be opened to the tourist from the Eastern States, which will bring throngs of summer travellers. It will then be fashionable to visit the Falls of St. Anthony, and to rave about the beauty of the Upper Mississippi, from which those are now cut off who do not care to go down the Ohio and ascend the Great River, and whose love of scenery is not strong enough to induce them to brave eighty or ninety miles of staging over a perilous and fatiguing road. Never was a railroad more needed, nor one which promised a surer or more continual product for the capital invested in its construction; so essential a link will it be in the great chain stretching from the Mississippi to the Hudson.

The first prairies on which you enter are perfectly level—a treeless, shrubless expanse, with groves like islands in the distance, and a line of woods on the verge; the space between much cut up by cultivated fields and farm-houses with flourishing gardens. Fine oak openings are seen at intervals every where. The grass, even on the prairies which had not been grazed over or mown, was little more than a foot high, and profusely sprinkled with pale yellow and flame-colored, or blue and pink flowers. Now and then the prairie squirrel or gopher leaps across the path. The shortness of the grass, owing in some measure to the late drought, much disappointed us in the first views of these "gardens of the desert," especially after ascending to a somewhat higher level, when we came into the region of the rolling prairies. Cultivation, too, has sadly marred the effect of these; one can scarcely conceive how much the sight of a distant corn patch, or field of wheat, or even a fence, or inclosure round a dwelling, takes away from the aspect of romantic wildness usually associated with the idea of a prairie of the West. Its vernal aspect, when the gold and crimson flowers contrast with the tender green, must be such as to inspire what Margaret Fuller called a "fairy land exultation," and there is moreover something in the feeling she describes, that she might continue a walk with any seven-leagued mode of conveyance, hundreds of miles without an obstacle. There is, too, a peculiar beauty in the sunset and moonlight, of the same kind with their loveliness at sea, and the clustering island groves are sheltering nooks for delicate romance; nevertheless, the idea expanded by the poetic dream is not filled by the reality. Who does not associate with the thought of a prairie the swaying of the wind, so that its fleet course may be traced by the bending of the reedy grass, or the tossing of the golden flowers, or the slow moving clouds, which

> "Sweep over with their shadows, and beneath
> The surface rolls and fluctuates to the eye:
> Dark hollows seem to glide along, and chase
> The sunny ridges—"?

Yet on the upland prairies this is rarely or never seen. The motion of tall grass would give to these plains much of the sublimity and magnificence of ocean, which now they resemble only in the grandeur of their vast extent, and the undulating outline defined against the far-off sky like the billowy swelling of the sea. The burning of the grass, which is done every year, presents a splendid spectacle, though less stupendous than the perilous and poetical conflagrations described by glowing pens. Several blackened patches showed where the dry grass had been recently burned.

At Prairie State Mills, about forty miles from Chicago, we came upon the Fox River, a low but graceful stream flowing through a pretty valley on the left, in which herds of cattle were grazing. This river follows us to Elgin, a flourishing business place, and disappears after many picturesque windings. Then comes the Heohwaukee and other smaller streams, and after passing a village or two, the train stopped at Cherry Valley, where the railway then terminated. Our progress had been slow, but we endeavored to console ourselves by observing the scenery. Miss C. counted eighty different species of plants in flower, which she duly noted in her journal, besides a number of sedges and grasses.

At Cherry Valley private vehicles and coaches were in readiness to convey travellers to their destination; those bound to Galena were consigned to the latter, and were soon jolting over roads, respecting which they were assured every few miles that they were "just passing over the worst." It will be a joyful era in civilization when those heavy, lumbering, leathery horrors are banished from the traveller's knowledge! Since our pilgrimage over the mountains of Virginia and the dusty highways of Tennessee, I had not seen one, and the aspect of four drawn up in file, to be filled by the victims ejected from the cars, was appalling enough, without the addition of a surly, dirty-looking Jehu on the driver's seat of each, whose grim visage and profane tongue checked on the instant the half-formed wish to occupy a seat on the outside. Into one of these purgatories we perforce climbed, and two of us, sighing, took our places on the back seat. It was soon crowded with rather a rough population; but who can blame petulance, under circumstances disagreeable enough to neutralize all the genial effects of Western atmosphere and custom! One woman with a child, who entered last, found a place on the front seat, and complained of her lot; whereat a tall, raw-boned amazon in a white sun-bonnet, who took up the largest third of the middle seat, with a grin meant to be gracious, desired me to change and go to the front. My declining to accommodate the new comer on the plea that I feared being made sick, drew down her indignation and that of the woman's husband and a pert little girl of about thirteen, who echoed whatever the others said, enforcing their axioms occasionally by a poke of her needle-like elbow into the sides of whoever she chanced to be near—the while changing her seat every three minutes. "I'm thankful *I* am not disobleeging!—You can have *my* seat any time." (She took care never to suit the action to the word.) "*I* am not fearful of sea-sickness."—"It's cur'ous how timid some folks is!" &c., keeping up a perpetual stream of talk, and mingling the most searching inquiries into the domestic affairs of her neighbors with a voluble autobiography and the private annals of sundry families of her acquaintance, in a manner that would have been ludicrous, had not the sharp and incessant din of her tongue been like daggers in our ears. She speered several questions at me, which were answered with repulsive monosyllables, and then she launched into remarks she meant to be applied, concerning the pride of "some folk, who thought themselves better than some other folk." It was a sensible mitigation of the nuisance, however, to learn that she was going no farther than Freeport.

Rockford, seven miles from Cherry Valley, is beautifully situated on Rock River, a noble stream which flows through the most picturesque part of Illinois. Miss Fuller speaks of it as flowing "sometimes through parks and lawns, then between high bluffs whose grassy ridges are covered with fine trees, or broken with crumbling stone that easily assumes the form of buttress, arch, and clustered columns. Along the face of such crumbling rocks swallows' nests are thick as cities, and eagles and deer do not disdain their summits." Bryant observes that the shores of this river unite the beauties of the Hudson and the Connecticut. Its course is through upland prairie, yet its banks are often bold, and sometimes perpendicular precipices or steep bluffs, rock-turreted, or covered with woods on the low lands. The prairies extend back of the bluffs, from the face of which clear springs gush out, and send their tribute to the river.

A stoppage was made here of an hour for dinner, fifty minutes of which were consumed in the preparation of the meal, leaving the passengers ten in which to eat it and secure their places in the crowded stages. Now came our fit again, and truly it seemed as if all things, including the roads and weather, had conspired to make this journey memorable in the record of the petty miseries of human life. The extreme heat was rendered more oppressive by a slight dampness in the air, and the road exhibited the phenomena of dangerous mud-holes combined with a stifling atmosphere of dust. Into these plunged ever and anon the cumbrous, shackling vehicle, and came out with a violent jerk, to the utter discomfort of the tumbling and grumbling passengers, above whose muttered plaints rose a shrill trio from the woman, whose name the amazon proclaimed to be Mrs. Johnson—her husband, and the hopeful girl, with loud exclamations from the strapping regulator of the movements and sessions of the coachful, who treated our hapless mother tongue with great cruelty. It was an omen of relief, at least from the overpowering heat, when the driver was seen to alight and encase himself in an India-rubber overcoat; and in about an hour the long desired shower came upon us. We had groaned at the dust, but alas, found the rain harder to endure; for it stayed with us, and without cooling the air, added both to the discomforts and dangers of the way. At Freeport a miserable supper was offered, with the like delay in preparing and hurry in dispatching; and then a night's travel was commenced, the like of which one may hope never to encounter again.

Our tormentor in the white sun-bonnet had disappeared—but her influence lingered; she had given whispered instructions, overheard by those interested, to the woman with the infant to go without her tea for the purpose of securing the back seat, and her husband took his place beside her, manfully resolved to do battle for the moiety of comfort it promised. M. quietly yielded to his intrusion on her rights, and edged herself into a corner on the front seat; the only place left was a segment of the back one, which must be filled, for there were nine inside, but which Mr. Johnson was sternly determined should *not* be occupied. The interference of the driver had to be invoked, and as the only alternative was for one of us to get out of the stage, the surly passenger was compelled to give up the point, and suffer the intrusion on the premises he claimed of one of the ladies he had dislodged. I mention this incident as a rare exception to the prevailing custom throughout the United States; at the West especially I have often seen men relinquish their seats to female passengers, but never before saw one turned out of her seat by a man. No selfish preparations, however, could procure an hour of balmy repose. The rain, which was still falling soft and warm, had reduced the prairie roads to their worst summer condition, and a long line of black mud, checkered by holes at one side or another, and now and then a tumble-down bridge, could be seen by the light of the lamps. But let no one imagine that the mere view can give the least idea of a prairie "slough," or mud-hole! You may see one deceitfully covered with green turf, and suspect no danger till your horses' feet, or one of your wheels, shall be sunk so far as to render recovery impossible without the aid of stakes and ropes brought to the rescue. The story of the pedestrian's cap moving just above the black ooze, while the rider and horse were below, appears no fable.

Then the mud—it is of a peculiar quality, coal-black, and tenacious as tar. After our coach had plunged and slipped along an hour or two, lurching almost to an overturn first on one side, then on another, the voice of the driver calling for a light—for he "could not see an inch, and never drove over this road before" —did not tend to reassure those disposed to think of accidents, particularly as the information was added, that a night seldom passed without some stage being overset. The pockets of cigar-smokers were searched for matches, but vain was the attempt to light the lamp, till the last match had been used. Presently the driver in front roared out to "take care of the bridge" which his wheels had just demolished; a caution withheld till ours were in the act of going over it, bringing the stage down with a swing from which it seemed impossible to recover it. Next our driver called in great alarm for help: one of the horses had slipped, and lay sprawling in the mud. A succession of such agreeable incidents during the whole night, kept before our minds the probability of having limbs broken, or of spending the rest of the hours of darkness on the lone, waste prairie, miles from any human habitation, with the wet grass for a couch. These not very exhilarating circumstances were rendered intolerable by the most shocking profanity on the part of the drivers. Ours kept up a soliloquy of oaths, and when an accident or a stoppage brought him into the fellowship of his companions, the concert of blasphemies was absolutely terrifying. Such conduct should never have been permitted by the directors of the road.

The summer of 1853 will probably put an end to similar experiences by finishing the railroad. We took the whole night to accomplish twenty-eight miles, and were glad to escape without any serious accident, though a score of times had we been forced to descend from the coach and wallow through the mud with our thin-soled gaiters coated thickly to the instep, the rain penetrating the destructible part of bonnets, and saturating crape shawls. On arriving at the customary breakfast-house, none of the woe-begone passengers seemed disposed to stop; and as there were no signs of preparation, none of the inmates being up, the driver consented to go on fourteen miles to the next halting place. The prairies passed over at this stage were the finest and wildest we had yet seen; boundless in extent save by the bending horizon, and rolling in majestic undulations. Not a tree or shrub could be seen for miles. Within fourteen miles of Galena that aspect of the country began to change; instead of sweeping prairies a ridge of elevated land presented itself, the summit of which commanded an extensive view of a beautiful and varied landscape, patches of woods, sloping fields, meadows, orchards, etc., all giving evidence of a rich soil and high cultivation. The broken country became bolder, and abrupt conical hills began to rise in front, to be scaled by stony and irregular roads matched nowhere except within seven miles of the Mammoth Cave, in Kentucky. More elevated ranges appeared in the distance. Here and there we came upon "mineral openings," through which descent is made by a windlass to the lead mines for which this region has long been so famous. The workmen were busily occupied around the openings, and wagons loaded with the smelted lead and rough ore were continually passing. Rugged heights of limestone rock, in castellated form, their crevices and summits covered with tangled vines, bushes and trees, rose before us, and after scaling and descending several steep hills, we entered Galena about noon.

IV.

At the first view, Galena appears a very rough-looking place, "jammed in" between rocky hills, on which a large portion of the town is built. The ranges of houses rising one above another, built on terraces, stand at irregular intervals, so that but a small part of the town can be seen at one view from any point in the vicinity. Miss C. observed that if the inhabitants were not well acquainted with their neighbors' affairs, it must be their own fault, "for everybody has somebody else overlooking him, and he himself cannot well help a similar inspection. A wag, describing the city, said it 'looked like a drove of sheep going down to water.'"

We stayed at the house of Capt. Gear, Miss C.'s uncle, one of the oldest citizens, and among the earliest pioneers of Illinois. His residence, which was formerly a trading house, is not far from the river bank, and commands a fine view. The kindness of our reception was the more grateful from our need of quiet, and most welcome was the Sabbath rest of the following day, when we attended service in the Episcopal Church, situated on a steep hillside. It was a novel amusement in the evenings to sit by the window and see rushing almost under it, with the noise made by the Western high-pressure boats, steamers so large as apparently to fill up the little river that skirts the city, and is now shrunken by the drought into half its accustomed limits. At night the appearance of these boats, lighted up and filled with lively passengers, is very picturesque. All that ascend or descend the Mississippi, stop at Galena. The "fast boats" make the trip to St. Paul and back in a little over three days, averaging two a week; but we were counselled to wait and take a slow boat in preference, that the scenery might be seen to better advantage. Our kind host, meantime, and several of his friends, volunteered to show us things worthy of note in this vicinity. Capt. Gear has been for many years interested in the larger boats plying from St. Louis, and in the lead mines which have enabled Galena for a long time to control the whole trade on the upper portion of the Mississippi. He removed hither about 1827, saw the growth of the place to a town of importance, and realized a large fortune in the diggings. A fine painting, by Stanley, which hangs in his parlor, represents at once the source of his wealth and influence, and a critical moment in his history. Three different times was he buried under the surface in digging, and as often rescued; the last time from a depth of sixty feet in the earth, and forty feet of water, escaping to the surface by the ladder which always stands in the shaft. He is a man of remarkable stature, with a strong and muscular frame, and the artist has him at full length, standing at the mouth of the pole, one arm resting on the curb of the windlass, and the other leaning on his shovel.*

It will be remembered that the whole region watered by the St. Lawrence, the great lakes, and the Upper Mississippi, was first visited by the Jesuits, and that their reports induced French traders to establish themselves at different points in the northwest. By their flexible manners they accommodated themselves to Indian habits, and many of the traders who married Indian women, continued faithful to them, while others deserted their partners as soon as they had amassed sufficient property to satisfy their cupidity, taking away their children, and teaching them to forget, in a more polished life, their early associations. The old residents here have many stories of matches made by white men with Indian women. Dr. Muir, who gave its name to Galena, had acquired his profession at Edinburgh, and was a young man of interesting manners and excellent character. At one time he was surgeon to the troops stationed at Fort Snelling. A handsome maiden of the Fox tribe dreamed one night that she saw him unmoor her canoe, paddle it over from the other side of the river, and come directly to her lodge. She knew, according to her superstitious belief, that he was to be her husband, and of course, such a prophecy soon works out its own fulfilment.

"Muir was true to this attachment until the sneers

* In this chapter I have made, by permission, extracts from the journal of my fellow-traveller—Miss Clark.

of his brother officers made him ashamed of it, and as he was then ordered with the company to Bellefontaine, a fort just above the junction of the Missouri and Mississippi, he took this opportunity to get rid of his dark-browed partner, not thinking she could ever find him, or if she should, that she would have it in her power to follow him. But love triumphs over every impediment. With her infant child the intrepid wife and mother started alone in her canoe, and persevering through all difficulties, safely at last reached the object of her heart's idolatry; but so much had she undergone in mind and body, that, to use her own expressive phraseology, laying her hand on her breast, 'When I got there, I was all perished away—so thin!'

"After a journey of about nine hundred miles, accomplished for his sake, he could no longer withstand her devotion, and to save further annoyance from his friends, Muir threw up his commission and commenced practice in Galena. His wife always presided at her own table, and at entertainments given to his friends, but never relinquished her native dress. Their eldest son was educated at the Cherokee College in the south, but on his return, while at Keokuk, then an Indian village, he fell into the hands of sharpers, who endeavored to defraud him of his lands; in a moment of indignation he tore up one of their false papers, and being threatened and pursued for this, fled up the river, where he was accidentally drowned. Dr. Muir died suddenly, and as he left no available means, his widow went down the river to search for Mrs. Farrar, who had received a request from Governor Clark, of Missouri, if possible to get possession of the two young children. Unfortunately they missed each other, and the widow, failing to find the person to whom she was willing to relinquish them, returned with her little boy and girl to her own tribe, too far to be recovered, where it was ultimately ascertained they died from exposure and starvation.

"Though an old trading post much earlier, Galena first attracted Eastern settlers about 1819, when among others, Duff Green was here with a company. In the winter of 1827 there were but fifteen white women in the place, all of whom were once present at a party. Mrs. Martha Miller, wife of John S. Miller, was the first white woman who came to Galena, and she died lately in California. The first crime remembered after Galena became an American settlement, '*except a hot-headed murder or so in the diggings*,' was that of a negro who was convicted of stealing a keg of lard in 1828, when there were about two thousand inhabitants in the diggings. The offender was sentenced to be whipped. They used to say that the punishment for such offences was putting the criminal in a canoe, with provisions for a short time, and setting him afloat down the river, where of course there was no settlement to land at.

"In 1833 Galena was quite a populous village, and now numbers about seven thousand. It is the great metropolis of the lead trade, and on its wharves may be seen piles of the smelted metal to the amount of many tons, laid up in bars ready for exportation.

"Lead mineral runs with the points of the compass —north or south in vein or sheet, and is sometimes found within a few feet of the surface. It has been worked to the depth of one hundred and twenty feet, which has generally taken it to the water. East and west the mineral lies in crevices, but seldom in sheets, and is found in openings and caves. The present price is twenty-six or twenty-eight dollars per thousand."

It is not a little remarkable to observe the prejudice in the minds of many travellers against Galena on account of the name of the useful little river which runs by it. Several passengers from Chicago put themselves to no little inconvenience to avoid stopping there, supposing the place haunted by fevers. "A rose by any other name would smell as sweet," but Galena seems doomed to suffer the penalty of an inappropriate cognomen, or rather a misapplication of a sound; for the fact is, that the river was named after a French trader, and is Fêvre, or Bean River, supposed by some to derive its name from the wild beans which abounded on its banks. The elevated and rocky site of the town would seem to indicate a particularly healthy location, and the report of residents confirms this conclusion. The rugged acclivities and abrupt ravines, when smoothed a little by culture, adorned with trees, and covered with more sightly buildings, will add an aspect of wildness and novelty to its beauty. Some of the houses are now accessible by narrow foot-bridges; there are the quaintest nooks for buildings imaginable, and the neatest cottages, nestled in verdure, are perched on hillsides, where they appear to much advantage. The great charm of the place is the generous spirit of social kindness which seems to prevail. Although we came almost strangers, we were made to feel at home at once by the most cordial of welcomes from numerous friends, and every thing possible was done to promote our enjoyment. Having seen something of the best society of the town, we departed with most agreeable recollections.

A party was made up one day for an excursion into Iowa, for the purpose of making discoveries in a cave said to have been found within six miles of Dubuque. One in that vicinity had been explored, and rifled of most of its beautiful lime formations; but this was entirely unknown. The drive of two miles and a half to the ferry was through a picturesque country, over winding ascents which disclosed the most pleasing views of luxuriant valleys, wooded ravines, and extensive tracts of cultivated land. From a considerable height we had the first view of the glorious Mississippi, lying far down between the hills. The river at the ferry appeared to be a mile in width, inclosing many lovely islands fringed by a thick growth of willows, or covered with oaks. The road winding onward from the Iowa side, crosses some strips of prairie land, and skirts hills whose conical peaks are crowned with rocky turrets. The woodland consists entirely of light timber, in scattered growth or openings of considerable extent, with grass of the brightest verdure underneath, giving the country the appearance of an old and cultivated region, and every where the surface of the earth is covered with rich vegetation. Continually on ascending an elevation, magnificent panoramic views were discovered, extending frequently more than twenty miles; the hills, rock-crowned as with ruined castles, rising range above range, the loftiest melting into the blue distance. The picture was enchanting as extensive; there were fields golden with harvest and tracts of standing corn, meadows and pasture land of the smoothest verdure, and woods where streaks of sunshine checkered the shade. Few farm-houses were to be seen; a circumstance rather surprising when the advanced improvement of the soil is considered. The distant view of Dubuque, lying along the river shore at the base of its hills, was very imposing.

At length we left the road, turning to the left, and after a number of inquiries and misgivings, in about a quarter of an hour came to the house of a farmer, the proprietor of the cave. It was a double log hut, connected by a shed, as many are built hereabouts, one division having fallen much to decay, and the whole dwelling bespeaking little of comfort, although the interior was scrupulously clean. A somewhat saturnine old man nodded to us at the fence, and gave us permission to alight; while his gentle and sad looking wife set us chairs out of doors, and fetched cool water for our refreshment. Some cold water was thrown, too, upon our enthusiasm about the cave; though the owner speedily got over his first impression, that we were nefarious hunters for "mineral;" a class he seemed to hold in as great fear as if his possession could have been wrested from him. He assured us there was no entrance for us; the place was not "fixed;" several men had given up the attempt to enter, and latterly he had refused to permit any visitors to approach it, under the apprehension that they might discover another entrance on the property of some of his neighbors, who would thus come in for a share of any native lead it might contain. We were resolved however to "proceed to a trial," and as a preliminary adjourned to the spring which gushed—a cool blessing—from under an ancient oak in a beautiful grove near at hand. Here a pic-nic repast was spread out, consisting of crackers, cake and cheese, and apples rosy with the glow of a southern sun; accompanied with draughts of cool water bubbling from the earth, more delicious than the choicest product of the vine.

The farmer awaited our return at his house, where his wife had laid out some calico wrappers more suitable than our light habiliments for a subterranean excursion. When these preparations were completed, the old man led the way across the fields to the opening of the cave. It had been discovered while digging for lead mineral, several shafts having been sunk in the vicinity. A wide hollow had been made by throwing up the earth, in the centre of which a hole appeared as large as a well. The farmer fetched a stout stick, and threw it across the opening, to which he tied a rope; those who ventured in were to descend some twenty feet perpendicularly, entering then a horizontal passage, so narrow and low as scarcely to permit one to crawl, working along with difficulty, regardless of mud beneath and dripping water above. It was too much of an adventure for women, and with regret we resigned the honor of pioneership to one abler and more courageous.

Dr. —— accordingly equipped himself, and taking a candle and box of matches, disappeared in the darkness, calling out repeatedly to us as he proceeded, till his voice sounded hollow and stifled, and was finally lost. The rest of the party sat dolefully perched on mossy seats, listening to the descriptions of the proprietor, who seemed to take a pleasure in stimulating our curiosity, now that there was no opportunity of gratifying it. He expatiated particularly on the beauty of a large white stalactite, resembling an equestrian statue, which stood at the entrance of one of the chambers, and gave it as his opinion, that the cave extended many miles underground in the direction of the Mississippi, and could be easily explored, when once the difficulties of entrance were overcome.

The heat became intolerable, and leaving the farmer to wait for the reappearance of our friend, we returned to the shelter of the cabin. The good dame had put every thing in the neatest order, spreading her newest patchwork quilts on the two beds that stood in the room which served for kitchen, parlor, and chamber, and was seated at her knitting work. We learned that she had been married but a short time, though advanced in years, and that a disagreement between the old man and her children by a former marriage, had deprived her of their companionship. It was easy to perceive that he was of a crooked and surly disposition, and that she suffered the grinding martyrdom of an ill-used wife. As the tale was drawn from her, little by little, by the sympathy expressed, a few tears stole down her pale cheek, which she quietly wiped away, and apologized for having been led to speak of her sorrows. How true it is, that every dwelling, however humble or isolated, has its story of dole, its material for romance! yet how blessed is the knowledge, that as from the dreariest abode the blue and sunbright arch of heaven may be seen, so spans all human woes the hope of eternal life through a Saviour's expiation and righteousness, and sheds its cheering light into the narrowest and darkest cell in which is imprisoned the soul affiliated to Infinite love!

Some hours passed, and each of the party began to feel uneasy; the old man told us the cave had not been entered in a year, and no one knew the present condition of its atmosphere. At last it was agreed that we should get the farmer to go in search of the missing, when the cry "he is coming" put an end to apprehension. We should hardly have recognized our adventurous underground traveller, so bedaubed was he with mud from head to foot; his dress was sadly torn, and his hands were scratched in breaking from the sides of the cave the various and beautiful snowwhite stalactites, a number of which he brought tied up in a handkerchief. He had not penetrated to the most remarkable recesses of the cave, nor seen its largest chambers, on account of the extreme difficulty of the passage, but had seen enough to show that it would richly reward the trouble of exploration.

Our drive homeward was of necessity a rapid one, for evening was approaching. While passing through an oak grove we observed Mr. C——, who rode in front, suddenly check his horse; and presently saw an enormous rattlesnake marching slowly across the road. M—— sprang from the carriage instantly, claiming the prize for her cabinet; and though it raised the warning rattle, and prepared for a fatal coil, Dr. —— soon dispatched and hung it to the back of the carriage.

The sunset glow was lingering on the dark, clear waters of the Mississippi, when we returned to the ferry and embarked in the horse-boat. The golden and purple clouds were reflected on its bosom; the shadows of the headlands and islands lay still in its depths, and the moon nearly at the full, was sailing in high heaven, as we stood gazing at the dark mass of "Tête des Morts," a promontory overhanging the waters a little distance up. The spot is noted in tradition as the scene of mortal strife between two hostile parties of Indians, one of which drove the other to the verge of the precipice and over it. From the other side we had a drive to Galena by moonlight, and found several friends who had been invited to meet us, expecting our arrival. The little incidents of the day afforded them much more amusement, probably, than the reader has found in them.

V.

THE new steamer Ben Campbell was appointed to leave Galena at eight o'clock, Wednesday morning, 28th July. Captain Orrin Smith, who usually commands the Nominee, and is one of the proprietors of this line of boats, was in command, and we congratulated ourselves on the circumstance, having heard much of him as an excellent man and a sincere Christian. It is said that he always respects the Sabbath, not suffering his boat to be in progress on that sacred day. Many parties who have gone up the river have mentioned him as a most desirable companion on such an excursion, and his graceful courtesy and cordial manners cannot fail to win the regard of all who have the good fortune to travel under his care. The boat rivalled in size and elegance of arrangement the Lake and Ohio steamers; the state-rooms were large, and generally furnished with double beds and wardrobes, and the fare was so excellent, that one was naturally at a loss to conceive how passengers could possibly be conveyed four hundred miles, lodged and fed sumptuously, and provided with attendance for four dollars each, less than one would have to pay at an ordinary hotel;

at a time, too, when the *furore* of competition was over, the decline in the waters having stopped the running of many first-class boats.

Punctuality to the time fixed is seldom observed by Western boats, and it was after ten when we went on board, accompanied by a number of friends who came to say farewell and promise a meeting in Minnesota. The other passengers came in slowly, and it was curious to contrast the quiet of departure with the noise and confusion of such an occasion in New-York. We took our seats on a shaded part of the guards, but were presently rather sternly reminded by a gentleman acquaintance, that we were "out of bounds;"—and he pointed at the same time to the line of carpeting dividing the ladies' from the dining cabin, his expression intimating that it was inexorable. I looked wistfully at the small aft windows which afforded the only lookout, and the number of ladies reclining on the velvet sofas and easy chairs, and stoutly refused to give up my chance of viewing the scenery for any masculine prejudices, unless the rules of the boat demanded the deprivation. Presently our excellent captain came by, and an appeal to him was answered by an assurance that the forward part of the boat afforded the best view, and he would have pleasant seats placed there for our accommodation. So, as in most political revolutions, the attempt at oppression was followed by the struggle which secured complete liberty. In due time, while our friends stood on the land, the boat dropped silently down the stream, whose gentle windings it followed for seven miles. Three miles from

Galena, a strip of bottom land divides it from the parent river, across which a channel might easily be cut. The channel of the Mississippi at the junction is very tortuous, and the islands numerous, reminding one of St. Mary's River. The scenery is of the softest and most pleasing description; there are grassy meadows and slopes, islands shady with oak groves and gently swelling hills, around which the steamer wound merrily; the shore becoming bolder after we left Dubuque, and wooded headlands of considerable height overlooking the water, with here and there a grassy plateau sprinkled with tall trees.

Dubuque, so named after an old French trader buried near, who had an ancient claim to the land, is a flourishing town of some five thousand inhabitants, lying at the foot of the hills opposite the line dividing Illinois from Wisconsin. It is wonderful to remember that thirty years ago there was scarce a settlement on this river above St. Louis, except trading-houses at long intervals. In 1824 it took forty days to ascend the Mississippi from St. Louis to Galena in a bateau. The author of "Sketches of Minnesota" describes the usual method of navigating the river at that time, "unless a chance breeze happened to fill the sails of their slender craft; *bushwhacking*, *cordeling*, or *warping*. In cordeling the men walked along the shore, and drew the boat by a rope attached to it. That method was impracticable in high water. Bushwhacking was accomplished by seizing hold of the bushes along the shore, and propelling the boat by that means. This method could occasionally be resorted to, but warping was often the only means by which a boat could be propelled against the current. In warping they had two sets of boats and lines. A man went ahead in a boat, attached one end of a line to a tree or some fixed object on the shore, and hastened back to the bateau. The men threw the line over their shoulders and walked to the stern of the boat. Each one as he arrived at the stern, dropped the line, ran back to the bow, and seized it again. In the mean time the other boat was engaged in attaching another line, and thus all hands were constantly engaged in 'dragging their slow length along.'"

Six miles above Dubuque, below a rocky bluff, is the landing of Sinapee, which it was once thought would rival Galena as the lead dépôt. Buena Vista landing and its vicinity afford beautiful views; the high, conical hills are turreted with rock, as if their summits were castle-crowned; and the fairy islands dotting the waters, and the range of bluffs thickly wooded from their tops to the water's edge, save the rocky projections, with the vast variety of shade in their foliage, form an exquisite picture. It is difficult to separate into its component parts the beauty which here fills the imagination, so as to convey an adequate impression to those who have never seen it.; for this reason one can have little satisfaction in any description of the wonders of the Upper Mississippi. I have not seen on this noble river any one piece of scenery which surpasses the finest on the Hudson. The charm consists in the fact that a succession of pictures is presented; and as soon as one magnificent view disappears another opens on the sight. This is continued for hundreds of miles—forming a range of scenery scarcely paralleled upon the continent. Now we sail in the shadow of frowning crags one hundred and fifty or two hundred feet in height, densely covered with woods, a rude lodge or hut peering out from the foliage at long intervals; now we skirt some luxuriant prairie, or watch the lazy progress of large rafts loaded with timber, floating under the rocky ledge bordering the water; and the disposition of the willow-fringed islands and the sweep of the country beyond is highly picturesque. Prairie du Chien is a few miles above the mouth of Wisconsin River, and seventy-five miles by land from Galena. Fort Crawford, built here in 1819 by Gen. Taylor, is now abandoned, and its dismantled building gleamed white in the silvery moonlight. The ancient trading-house, half destroyed, is not a very sightly ruin. The town extends over a beautiful prairie, and is one of the oldest Western settlements. It is associated with romantic incidents of Indian trade and warfare. Here commences the loveliest scenery of the Mississippi.

The water was lower at this time than it had been for many years, but the boats are so constructed that their bow can touch the shore where a canoe could but just keep afloat. Bad Axe River has given a name to the battle-ground some miles below its mouth, on which was fought the battle between the United States troops and the Sauks and Foxes, under Black Hawk. At Prairie de La Crosse is a superb view of the heights further up, partially wooded and checkered by the play of sunshine and shadow. A sudden and welcome shower here came upon us, the large drops dancing on the water, and cooling the air, which had been of burning heat. Some crevices resembling caverns may be seen as we approach, half way up the cliff, and the rocks rising tower-like from their summit, and the green islands clustering at their feet, combine grandeur with beauty. The rocky face of this lofty range is more thinly covered with woods, and here and there a bright stream flings itself down. The character of the woods in this part of Minnesota is much the same with those of Iowa; they consist of a scattered growth of oaks, so low as to resemble orchard trees, with little or no underwood, and a rich carpeting of wild grass; unlike the primeval forests of the Eastern States, and looking rather like a country that has been inhabited and deserted, and is partially grown wild again, than a region newly redeemed from Indian possession, and actually inhabited almost exclusively by the wild savage. There appears an inconsistency between its smooth and cultivated aspect and the rude character of the pioneer huts seen occasionally, or the primitive Indian lodges scattered at intervals. A sweeping range of bluffs here begins on the Wisconsin side, their rugged summits crowned with discolored masses of rock.

This prairie was noted as a place of resort for the Indians, who came to play their favorite games. Their place has been taken by enterprising German and French settlers. A man was here arrested and brought on board, who had escaped from St. Paul some days before, having murdered his wife. The officers had tracked him thither, and were now taking him back to prison. He was permitted to sit on the forward deck, under guard, and had soon a crowd about him, listening to his account of the transaction. The fellow had a look of sullen desperation, under which some degree of fear was concealed, and seemed desirous of gaining sympathy. It was said this was the first murder of a white person committed in Minnesota Territory.

At several points the heights form an extensive amphitheatre, the river bending to wind through the valley, which expands to a considerable width. Opposite the mouth of Black River, at the base of a mountain, is the site of the new town of Dahcotah, on the Minnesota side. Above it rises a towering peak in the form of a sharp cone. A few scattered houses may be seen, most of them destitute of shade, though a beautiful grove is just at hand. There may be noticed the common red cedar, the first evergreen apparent, mingled with the bright green of the summer foliage. The steep bluffs are grassy to their summits, and partially covered with burr-oak orchards, a broad level plain of the productive soil extending five or six miles back. Frowning ledges of rock, tufted with foliage, give the heights an aspect of savage grandeur. The islands are low and wooded thickly with cotton-wood, willow trees, and shrubbery, covered with vines.

Hereabouts is the point where Lester, the sheriff of Crawford County, in Wisconsin, on his return from Lake Pepin to Prairie du Chien, was shot by an Indian, who hailed and asked him for food. His body floated ten miles below, and was found by the deputy, from whom I received the account, among the willows. Some Indian chiefs being captured as hostages, the murderer was delivered up by the savages, but was acquitted for want of evidence, the half-breed who had seen the murder being unable to identify him with sufficient accuracy. This sad example of the troubles often occurring on the frontier, took place in 1844, just below "Catlin's Rock," so called from the artist who carved his name on the ledge. The shore is here very romantic, girdled with a ledge of rock in which the water has worn shallow caverns alternated with ragged points covered with groves of burr-oak. The picture extends just above Mount Trombolo into one of the finest views on the river. This may be a corruption of "*mont qui trempe à l'eau*," and is a high rocky island, rising steeply from the water, and conspicuously detached from the eminences surrounding it. The magnificent range of conical heights on either side, towering to an elevation of from three to five hundred feet, stretches as far northward as the eye can reach, forming a majestic amphitheatre of peaks; and the prairie on the Wisconsin side extends to the Trombolo River. Two or three shadowy islands dropped in the centre of the foreground add to the beauty of the scene, than which none more full of sublimity and loveliness ever employed an artist's pencil.

Bonnel's Landing is the site of another new town and the commencement of Wabasha Prairie. There is a road by land hence to Traverse des Sioux, about one hundred miles distant, through a luxuriant country. The grassy slope is sprinkled with the shadows of oaks, and cattle were grazing on the rich wild grass.

I noticed a recognition here, on board the boat, which much pleased me. A well dressed man accosted a gentleman by the name of Oakes, a resident of St. Paul, mentioned his own name, and begged to express his gratitude for kindness rendered years before in circumstances of distress. "You would not probably know me for the same," he continued, "for I was in rags when you assisted me;" and I thought the incident and his grateful tones embodied one of the touching romances of real life.

A curious sugarloaf hill, looking as if split down through the middle, here attracts attention among the bluish peaks in the distance. It has its exact counterpart on the shore of Lake Pepin; and the legend is, that the entire mountain once belonged to two Indian deities, who quarrelling, at length they parted company, agreed to divide the mountain, and one brought his half to Wabasha. Further up, the bluffs recede, and the beautiful prairie is bounded by them in a semicircular range, from half a mile to three miles in width, and skirted by a sluggish stream called a "slough" in western parlance. There is an Indian settlement not far off, and a farm-house where an old Indian was established by Government after the treaty of 1837, for the cultivation of land on the east side of the river.

It is said that when the Winnebagoes on their way to their new homes, reached Wabasha Prairie, they refused to proceed further, and throwing off their blankets, assumed a warlike attitude, yelling, and brandishing their tomahawks with warlike gestures, as if the beautiful scene had called up recollections that stung them to temporary madness. The prairie was named after the chief of a band of Sioux, whose *tepees* were not long since scattered at its extremity. It was now sprinkled with a number of rude "shanties" thrown up for the temporary accommodation of a colony of pioneers from New-York, who had come several weeks before, and laid out a village in the neighborhood. One lady, whose husband was among them, merely on a visit, however, came on the boat from Galena, and landed here, intending to join him. She looked as cheerful as if she thought a pioneer expedition a pleasant frolic, and took her way across the prairie, accompanied only by a few rustic children, while a few barrels of flour, and boxes of live fowl, were put ashore for the use of the emigrants. There is a white settlement some six miles back. The rough cabins of new-comers along the shore, built of logs, with mud and stick chimneys on the outside, are often placed high up the hills, and present a curious sight in these park-like oak woods, which would be in keeping with a cottage ornée, or elegant country-seat.

There is a beautiful view below Whitewater, of a range of promontories and islets dotting the broad river in most picturesque disposition. At Wabasha village those who wished to see savage life were amused by the pranks of the half naked Indian children, who ran into the waves raised by the steamboat wheels, flinging the water about with exulting shouts, while a hard-featured savage, with a yell as of defiance, shot his canoe directly across the channel before the boat.

This village is on a tract belonging still to a company of Sioux half-breeds, the treaty for its sale not having been ratified by Government. A few Canadians live there, and some educated half-breeds, whose houses are neatly painted and surrounded with pretty gardens. These are interspersed with the Sioux lodges, or *tepees* as they are called, built by covering poles with skins: and the narrow canoes made by hollowing out logs, by savages of that tribe, who have not the birch bark used by the Chippewa race, line the shore. At a distance a white flag waving over an inclosure denotes the burial-ground, and an old frame house, surmounted by a cross, is the Catholic church. This is near the mouth of the Chippewa River, and four miles below the commencement of Lake Pepin, that beautiful expansion of the river of which so much has been said in description and legend.

The islands here disappear, and the increased swell of the waters shows greater volume and depth. Near the entrance, which is guarded by a rocky promontory, is a plateau on the Wisconsin side, where many years since a war party of Chippewas, coming to look for Sioux, killed several white traders. There is another legend connected with this locality, to which is said to be owing the song of the Indian sacred medicine dance. A Sauk and a Sioux Indian were together in a canoe, when they heard a strain of wild music, and at the same time felt the canoe upborne from the water by the local deity. The Sauk, affrighted, gave a scream, when it sank suddenly, and he was drowned; the other, beginning to repeat the song, felt the boat rise again, and the music continued, which he remembered, and taught his people. This tradition is firmly believed among the savages. There is hardly a locality on the shores of the Upper Mississippi, which is not associated with some Indian legend or historical incident.

The sun gave us his farewell in a purple and golden panoply behind the bluffs, and the full moon rose as we glided over these storied waters, bounded on all sides by their magnificent and lofty rampart. Such a scene, blended with associations so romantic, might well make an artist of the least susceptible; yet there were some on board who withstood all the enchantments of this unrivalled scenery. Some of the women hardly quitted the ladies' saloon during the voyage, passing their time in reading novels and arraying their persons, changing their dress several times a day. It appears to be the custom among female passengers in this region, to adopt a style of dress suited rather to a ball-room, than the accidents of a journey. Thin tissues and muslins like "woven air" were evidently in favor, and many wore these delicate fabrics cut with low-necked waist and short sleeves, trusting to lace shawls or embroidered Swiss mantillas for protection against the breezes which in the evening and morning now became cool and bracing. A homely contrast was offered by our weather-defying ginghams and delaines, and sooth to say, we did not envy the cabined seclusion to which others were condemned by the necessity of keeping fresh their elegant costumes.

One party of three or four, the family of a Boniface in the lead region, was the admiration of the rest, so various and beautiful were the morning, noon, dinner, and evening dresses they successively displayed. The largest rocking chairs were relinquished to them by common consent, and a nice lunch served, chiefly for their convenience, every morning at eleven in the saloon; a repast which seemed to our unsophisticated habits rather superfluous, as a sumptuous dinner was set forth at one o'clock.

"Maiden's Rock" towers some two hundred feet above the water, a gray, stark, frowning precipice, looking grand and savage in relief against the moonlit sky. Nearly opposite is the residence of a celebrated trader, who lives in baronial style, and was then inclosing a park, with pickets, for his deer. He married a half-breed of the country, and may be considered to represent both the savage and civilized condition. The tradition connected with the Maiden's Rock is so variously told that you seldom hear the same version. A lady who had lived many years at Fort Snelling, and received the story from the lips of an aged Dakota, who said he had been an eye-witness of the scene, informed me that a young Sioux girl had been accustomed to meet her lover, who was hated by her kindred, near this spot; displaying a token of security, when the lover's canoe might be seen shooting rapidly across the lake, while the dark-haired maiden stood on the bank. These stolen interviews at length became known to her relatives, who had already betrothed her to another. The maiden promised her brave to fly with him, and watched for an opportunity. One evening a hunting party of her people was encamped not far from the lake. She was with them, filled with anxiety and terror, for she knew her beloved would come that very night to seek an interview with her. She saw his canoe gliding across the waters; the others, too, caught the sight, and in desperation the young girl clambered to the summit of the bluff, with frantic gestures striving to warn her lover of his danger. The young chief, perhaps, mistook her meaning; he came swiftly to the eastern shore, and as he met his fate at the hands of his foes, a fearful shriek from the cliff mingled with the yell of savage vengeance, and the hapless maiden, springing from the sheer verge, fell a corpse at the base of the bluff.

Behind the lofty bluffs inclosing Lake Pepin stretches an extensive plain, as is usual in the West, level with the summit of the heights. This expanse of prairie is interspersed with oak groves, and beautiful in its grassy undulations. The tributaries to the Mississippi flow through a deep channel cut in this plain, guarded also by peering and precipitous bluffs.

The Dakota village of Red Wing is on the Minnesota shore, not far from the lake, and near the mouth of Cannon River. The St. Croix River enters the Mississippi at Point Douglas, a fine site for a town, commanding a view of the river and the lake of St. Croix. The surrounding country is rapidly filling with an industrious farming population. Red Rock, six miles below St. Paul, is so called from a boulder painted red lying near the shore, said to be worshipped by the savages.

Early in the morning we passed Kaposia, or "Little Crow," a Sioux village of considerable size. The houses, built of strips of oak bark, laid across stakes pitched like tents, were arranged in somewhat regular order on the rising ground, which overlooked the water. A number of conical *tepées* covered with skins, were scattered between; the latter being the favorite Indian residence for winter; and though smaller than the Chippewa wigwams, whole families will live in one of them. The peculiar narrow and crank "dug out" canoes used by this people, lined the beach in great numbers, tipped with red at the ends: some of them half filled with squaws and children, who must have an art of balancing themselves unknown to civilized beings, or they could not fail to be overset. A green and shadowy gorge, opened back between the hills; and on the heights in the distance were rude scaffoldings, surmounted by a white cloth or blanket, the covering of the Sioux dead; for it is their custom, instead of burying the bodies of their deceased friends, to expose them in this manner in the open air for weeks. Their superstition appears to dread the pressure of earth, and they fancy that their dead can see what is passing around them. The bodies are generally buried after a few months, though sometimes left longer on the scaffold. Usually white flags wave near the spot, denoting that it is sacred ground.

Three or four Indians came on board here, dressed with some attempt at display, but hideously dirty. Their pipes and tomahawks were in one piece, the handle of the weapon serving for a pipe-stem. They preferred a lounge amidst the freight in the "lighter" alongside to a seat among the curious passengers; but one made amends for their want of sociability by giving us an air on his rudely constructed flute, assuming a sentimental attitude, for this is their fashion of lovemaking.

The plateau near the great bend of the Mississippi a little below St. Paul, is the scene of a bloody massacre of several Sioux by a party of Chippewas who surprised them while intoxicated. One of them shot a trader's half-breed wife, and the slicing off the head of her child so quickly that the body stood erect for a moment, was the signal for a general onset. A pretty ravine here conducts the mighty river onward, close to which we were doomed to rest longer than we had anticipated; for the steamer being of larger size than the boats ascending the river, and the water extraordinarily low, a sand-bar at the point presented a barrier that could not be overcome till the cattle had been put ashore, and much of the freight removed into a barge alongside. This was within view of the town, the white houses of which showed imposingly on the bluff. It is usually called "Pigs Eye" bar, a name given to a small settlement of French and Canadians, it is said on account of a remarkable expression in the face of its first inhabitant, who had but one eye. For the remainder of the summer this place assumed to itself the honor contended for by St. Paul and St Anthony, of being the acknowledged head of navigation. The boat lay here some hours, and it was nearly twelve before the impediment was got over. We were to land a little after noon, but Captain Smith had given orders to have dinner prepared an hour before the time; a custom usual with him, it was observed; for he "never liked to send away his passengers hungry." In view of the extreme cheapness of travelling on this route, and the superior quality of the fare, this incident strikingly illustrates Western liberality.

In due time we came triumphantly into port, landing at the base of a bluff, the top and sides of which were crowded with idlers—several Indians among them. There were carriages as luxurious as New-York affords, stages for St. Anthony, and omnibuses for the different hotels, in waiting. Our stately dames had arrayed themselves in rich silks, with embroidered shawls and bonnets of delicate gauze, to enter the capital of Minnesota. We proceeded to the Rice House, where Miss C. was dismayed by the information that both families of the friends whose hospitality she expected to enjoy had the varioloid; but we found excellent quarters in the hotel. Its proprietor is Mr. Daniels, a gentleman of intelligence and polished manners. He had just finished a splendid house when it was destroyed by fire. Much of the furniture, which is new and elegant, was saved and transferred to the present building.

Our after experience afforded us much amusement in seeing the excitement produced throughout the town by a new arrival. Truly it was picturesque and illustrative! An unusual bustle pervades the streets; men are hurrying to and fro; voices are heard in some confusion; there is the rumbling of carriage wheels, and the call of drivers. A light line of smoke is seen curling over the mass of foliage on a distant bluff; a steamboat is coming! What hopes and fears, what thrilling emotions are called up by the event in the breasts of many! The noise increases; people hasten towards the landing to greet friends or hear the news; the neatly covered carriage of the Rice House drives rapidly down, to secure a place on the landing and bring up travellers to comfortable quarters. But alas! the smoke has become suddenly stationary; the boat has struck the formidable bar! One by one the stragglers depart; but the carriages wait—and after the delay of an hour or two, the boat generally arrives at the landing.

VI.

THE situation of St. Paul is unsurpassed for beauty of view. It stands on a bluff eighty or ninety feet high, overlooking the winding Mississippi, now diminished to an ordinary stream by the lowness of its waters; the plain is just undulating and broken enough to save it from the uniformity of a perfect level, and present an agreeable variety in the appearance of the town. The streets are laid out regularly, and are of ample width, not built up as yet with substantial houses, but rapidly improving. Indeed it is surprising how much has been accomplished within three years, at the beginning of which there were about a dozen log houses, and a small log Catholic chapel, from which the town afterwards took its name. Now the number of inhabitants is twenty-five hundred or more, and there is an air of brisk progress and life about the place, which with its advantages of location, and the increasing resources of the country, will, in a short time, make it a city of importance. In portions of the town not yet improved by buildings, it is curious to see the primitive undergrowth of the woods, and even trees, left. In walking from the Rice House to the residence of the

Governor, in what may be called the heart of the town, we passed through quite a little forest; crossed a mountain-stream flinging itself impetuously down the hillside, and saw a bear's cub at play—an incident in keeping with the scene. Some very handsome buildings are in progress; the new State-House, the Catholic church, and other public edifices. Five churches are completed and one more is in progress. It is two years since the Episcopal mission was established, and the fact was stated to Miss C—— that three clergymen with their students, visit once in three weeks every neighborhood from Point Douglas to Fort Ripley, and thence to the Falls of St. Croix, maintaining service every Sunday at St. Paul and St. Anthony. The mission house in St. Paul is a neat Gothic cottage embowered in trees, and the church a handsome building in the Gothic style of architecture. Mr. Breck, much to the regret of the parish, had just accepted an invitation from the Chippewas to remove the central point of his labors to Gull Lake. Rev. Edward D. Neill, the pastor of the Presbyterian congregation, is a highly intelligent gentleman, and learned in the reminiscences and traditions of the Territory, being secretary of the Historical Society of Minnesota. His library includes almost every thing relating to its history within two centuries, from the time when Father Hennepin first broke the silence of these northern wilds with a white man's voice, to the expeditions of Cass and Schoolcraft, Nicollet and Pike in later years. He presented M—— with several numbers of the "Dakota Friend," the first religious newspaper published in the Northwest, and printed in English and the Sioux language. Some of its best articles from his pen, record curious customs of the Dakota race, with biographies of those earliest settlers of the country, known as "*Coureurs des bois.*"*

The editor of the first newspaper published here, facetiously announced it as "The Epistle of St. Paul," but afterwards more decorously called it "The Minnesota Pioneer." Its first number appeared in April 1849.

The prospects of the missions on the Mississippi and Minnesota Rivers are at present discouraging, but the laborers in that field, who have been long with the Sioux, work on with prayer and self-denial, unwilling to leave the people with whom they have cast their lot, and looking in faith for the hour when spiritual light will break upon the benighted race. It is thought that, reluctant to lose what little has been gained, they will cling to the fortunes of the Dakotas,

* Miss C——, who furnished me with this information, says, quoting Mr. Neill: So little do the Dakotas know of law, that no words in their tongue can be found, which will accurately convey that passage in the prayer of our Lord—"Thy kingdom come,—Thy will be done." Gov. Ramsey holds this language: "As a political community the Dakotas live almost without law. Slight, indeed, among all the tribes of the Northwest, is the influence of their chiefs; the braves, who constitute a sort of aristocratic estate, keep them in awe, and through the depression of fear, the chiefs hesitate in council to express an independent opinion. For this reason, upon the occasion of transacting important business, they always insist upon the presence of a large number of their people. Should they sign a treaty, or do any act binding upon their tribe, contrary to popular approbation, it is very probable their lives would be the forfeit."

when they leave their ancient homes, and take up their journey towards the Rocky Mountains. The train from the Red River had just brought news of the murder of a young teacher sent last year from St. Paul to the Selkirk settlement, by a party of Yankton Sioux, who are hostile to the inhabitants of Pembina, it is supposed on account of their relations to the Chippewas. It is well known that there has been a feud from time immemorial between the Sioux and Chippewas, two of the most powerful Indian nations in the territories of the United States.

M—— had an interview with the Roman Catholic Bishop of the diocese of Minnesota, Rt. Rev. Joseph Cretin, who informed her there were about nine hundred members of that church in the Territory. There are Catholic schools for boys and for girls, and one for both sexes at the Episcopal Mission house.

The city of St. Paul must be the central point of business for the Northwest, from Lacquiparle to the Missouri, to the Red River of the North, and thence to Lake Superior. Its growth has been one of unexampled rapidity, and fortunately for its prosperity and the well-being of its citizens, the Maine Liquor law is now in force throughout the Territory. The expenses of living are much more moderate than could be supposed possible, in view of the fact that all supplies must be brought up the river, and that navigation is suspended for a large portion of the year. Board at the best hotel costs but a dollar and a half a day, and from three to five dollars a week. Rent is high, for the houses are too few to accommodate the increasing numbers who want them, and labor commands excellent wages, a man receiving twenty, and a female servant from ten to twelve dollars per month. Mechanics can earn two dollars or more a day.

The curious blending of savage and civilized life attracted our attention. The lodges of the Dakotas had vanished from the opposite shore, those lands having passed from their possession, but their canoes yet glided over the waters of the Mississippi, and we met them whenever we stepped outside the door; nay, they would almost every day enter the parlors of the hotel, seat themselves unceremoniously, and remain for hours, seldom speaking unless addressed, and always intimating that they did not understand English. They never answer discourteously, however, to a salutation in their own musical tongue. The men are generally painted elaborately, some of them showing visages of the brightest flame color, streaked with black, blue or yellow. They usually wear white or scarlet blankets striped with black, and have their heads decorated with eagle feathers—badges of victory—for each represents the scalp of a Chippewa. Their ornaments of shells, pewter, brass, &c., are of every possible variety; some of the braves have bells fastened to their leggins, or perfume bottles tied to the ends of their braided locks; and now and then a warrior clad in skins sports a necklace of bear's claws about his neck. Any attempt to give a general idea of their costume, when every one loads himself with all the tinsel and ragged finery he can find, would be perfectly useless. The women carry their pappooses, like the

Chippewas, on their backs, strapped to a board, or dangling over their dirty blankets, seemingly insensible to the fatigue of the mother's careless walk, or the heat of the sun shining directly in their faces. These Indians wander through the streets for the purpose of begging, trading, or amusing themselves, and return in the evening to their distant places of encampment. A cousin of mine, who had much veneration for the aboriginal race, on stepping ashore not long since from the steamboat, accosted a dignified looking chief, and was answered by a somewhat prolonged speech in the deep, harmonious Dakota tones. Supposing it a poetical apostrophe, he begged an explanation of an interpreter, and was informed that the chief was asking him for an apple! The Winnebagoes are more cleanly and respectable looking: their tribe is said to be the richest on the continent, for there are only about twenty-five hundred of them, and their payments from government amount to some ninety thousand dollars. At St. Anthony a handsome young girl of that tribe, who was said to have an American lover, was in the habit of coming every day into the parlor of the hotel, and talking volubly to us; pretending she could not understand us, though her blushes and laughter often betrayed her knowledge of what we were speaking about. She presented me with a string of glass beads, and another lady with a pewter ring, in token of remembrance.

In the afternoon we walked about the city, which is divided into the upper and lower town. There is a landing for steamboats in each. The edge of the high bluff in the centre of the town, affords a fine promenade, with one of the most superb views in the world, and ought never to have been cut up into building lots.

Early the next morning, Gov. R. and his beautiful and accomplished wife accompanied us in a drive to "Spring Cave," about two miles up the river. A rustic pavilion stands in the woods, where lights can be procured to enter the cave. A footbridge over a narrow ravine, and a winding path descending into its depths and leading through it a short distance, brought us to the entrance. This is in a small amphitheatre of white sandstone cliffs resembling loaf-sugar; along their base on one side rushed a stream of the clearest water that ever flowed, issuing from the cave, and dashing merrily along over the snow-white sand, its transparent waters sparkling like a shower of diamonds. After a lively progress through the shaded ravine, it skirts the rich bottom land, and hastens to carry its tribute to the Mississippi. The arched entrance, with its pillars of sand, and the bright streamlet gushing out at one side, was beautiful as a marble temple. You enter a winding passage, and soon lose the daylight, the stream becoming larger and more boisterous, till on arriving at a narrower rift, a roar is heard like that of a cataract concealed in the bowels of the earth.

Those who do not mind wet feet and soiled dress may proceed, ascending the rocks, to several spacious chambers, and see the rapids and the waterfall; thence onward the passage narrows again, and our penetration did not extend further. No doubt the beauty of the place would reward search; but as there was no prospect of finding any trophies in the way of stalactites, we left the honor to more persevering travellers.

Returning down the river, in about half a mile we meet this pretty stream in a new freak of gayety. A miniature waterfall flashes through the depths of a narrow dell, making thirteen successive shoots in a winding course, each falling into a lovely basin several feet in depth, which serves for a bathing-place, curtained by a drapery of woods. This little cascade is closely embowered in foliage of vivid green, and its picturesque beauty makes up for the want of grandeur. It is a lovely spot to spend a summer morning or afternoon.

The view of the country in this drive was a delicious one; every feature that can give varied beauty to a landscape was there, and one could not help wondering at the ease with which this fertile and delightful land can be subdued to yield the choicest products of cultivation. At present it is said the most profitable crop is potatoes, but we were assured by those who know more about farming than ourselves, that the soil is excellent for agricultural purposes. The salubrious climate, and bracing air, invigorate the human frame for both physical and mental exertion. In winter we are told, the stillness and dryness of the atmosphere enable one to endure with comfort a degree of cold that would be intolerable in St. Louis. With all the encouragement to emigration, it cannot be wondered at that every steamboat comes laden with new settlers. In a few years the tall bluffs that encircle St. Paul, inclosing the plain as in an amphitheatre, may be sprinkled with country residences, boasting more advantages of location than many of the proudest European villas.

One of our party thus described a view of the town and its vicinity from the residence of Mr. H. M. Rice, on a bluff about a mile to the west. "To our left lay the town, climbing the gently rising slopes, some of the houses perched on the extreme ascent, and the river, like a sparkling line of silver, curling around the base of all. In the southeast is a mass of green trees and foliage, and all along the horizon, as far as the eye can reach, it rests upon wooded eminences. To the south is the rich bottom-land of the Mississippi, sprinkled over with burr oaks—the kind most abundant in this part of Minnesota, looking like the apple trees of an orchard, disposed, as is usual, about the houses situated among them.

"A clear spring just on the hill side, bursting from its green brink, goes bounding down, and you may trace its course by the richer growth and hue of the velvet turf that spreads out like a carpet through the valley. On the west is the aspiring little town of Mendota, with its clustering white tenements, and though we cannot see it, we know that just above is Fort Snelling, where the prairie, shaded to a paler green, meets and mingles with the blue of the sky. Stretching off in the rear, is a beautiful opening, through which winds to St. Paul a delightful road, all the way smooth and firm as a floor."

The opposite shore of the Mississippi is still called

"the Sioux country," as it was in reality before last year's treaty, and is still by partial occupation, notwithstanding the flood of emigration that has been let loose this season. The Sioux and Winnebagoes who are seen wandering in and about the town, have their lodging places on the prairie or in the woods in the vicinity, where a few kettles and mouldering embers mark their place of encampment. They live chiefly on the fish and game they procure. M—— and I, while hunting cornelians on the Mississippi shore, with some others, amused ourselves with watching a Sioux woman cooking a heron one of the savages had captured. She built a fire by a stump, brought about a quart of water from the river and washed the bird as she divided it, placing the fragments, after a very slight washing, over the fire to stew. The claws and entrails she roasted and took to her companions in a canoe, to eat as choice morsels, while the supper was in preparation.

The condition of these wild Indians, driven from their ancient homes by the encroachment of civilization, is pitiable enough, and it must sadden the philanthropist and the Christian, to see the hopeless darkness and misery which seems to be their lot. The remedy must be provided by judicious legislation and patient perseverance in the work of doing good. The system of annual payments in money is an unfortunate one for them, inducing them to neglect making any provision for themselves, and leaving them, simple and credulous as they are, to the host of unprincipled traders who obtain their money by offering tempting gewgaws at an extravagant price. One well acquainted with their habits—Nathaniel McLean—says: "The views of most of those who have lived the longest among the Indians agree in one respect, that is, that no great or beneficial change can take place in their condition until the general government has made them amenable to local laws—laws which will punish the evil disposed, and secure the industrious in their property and individual rights, and thereby give them greater inducements to acquire property, and with it those many and increasing wants, which are not only the consequence, but the safeguard of civilization. Laws of this nature would also strike at the very root of one of the greatest evils which exist among them—their system of communism. It retards every thing like progress in the desire of bettering their condition. The most energetic and well disposed cannot rise above the vagabond and worthless. Indeed they are generally the best off who do the least, if they have a tact for begging or keeping their neighbors in apprehension. If the Indians could once be made industrious, the greatest difficulty would be surmounted. How then can this be accomplished, unless each man is secured the fruits of his labor? and that can only be effected by the legislative enactment of the general government.

"The present system of farming, it is now admitted by most persons, is entirely wrong. It surely never was the intention to labor for the Indians, instead of teaching and showing them how labor was to be done. Perhaps, in this respect, no great change can be effected with the old men and grown up persons of the present generation, but a wide field will doubtless be opened for the advancement of the young and rising generation, by means of manual labor schools. With the Indian race, perhaps more than any other, industry should go hand in hand with mental culture. It is useless to talk of regeneration and change of heart, so long as they are permitted to prowl about, a set of lazy, listless vagabonds. In that state occasional bursts of excitement are absolute necessities of existence. The hunter's life supplies this, and it is antagonistic to any thing like quiet industry, or even the first approach to civilization."

VII.

THE best thing visitors can do, after establishing themselves at the Rice House, and taking a survey of the curiosities of St. Paul, is to secure places in one of Willoughby and Powers' stages for what is called "the grand tour." This line runs three times a day between St. Paul and St. Anthony, and some are always at the landing on the arrival of the boats, to serve the convenience of passengers who wish to accomplish speedily what they have to do. They are new and handsome coaches, and the drivers are invariably civil and obliging. To accommodate any party desiring to make the excursion, they will make the tour referred to; driving first to St. Anthony and allowing time for a view of the different falls; then crossing the river and prairie to Lakes Harriet and Calhoun, the passengers taking a picnic dinner on the shore; thence to the Minneha-ha Falls and Fort Snelling, and by the Spring Cave to St. Paul, arriving in time for the visitors, if in haste, to return with the boat down the river.

We were summoned from our pastime of looking at the Indians by the stage horn, and found it waiting for us, nearly filled with passengers. Two of us took places on the top of the coach, the seats being well secured, and affording a splendid view of the country. A backwoods-looking, but civil man came up, and drew back when he found the inside full, and three besides the driver, perched aloft. We would not however permit his courtesy to deprive him of a place. He informed us he had been a passenger on board the "Ben Campbell," and had observed our party; but "did not like to intrude" on our notice, as he did not happen to be "dressed for society." He had a deal of the nasal twang of Yankeedom, and his phraseology was decidedly primitive, yet he showed much intelligence, and made some very sensible remarks on the country. He gave us to understand that he was seeking a location for a "new home," having obtained his wife's consent to remove if he could buy land that afforded a chance for making a fortune; yet he, as the driver afterwards said, was worth a hundred thousand dollars already. The solution of the mystery was easily given by himself. "The universal cry is 'more money,' and while I am in the meridian of life, I want to create an independence for my children." With all his rough exterior, he seemed to possess an extensive knowledge of literature; criticized the poetry of Dryden, Pope, and other English classics, and compared with them the poetry of Bryant, Longfellow, and a number of American bards, in a manner that showed he had read and appreciated them. If to be spoken of by the workmen in the mines, or to have a well thumbed copy of one's poems in a kitchen window, be the truest fame, to be quoted by a land hunter on the top of a Minnesota stage is certainly something.

After leaving St. Paul, you cross a fine breadth of prairie land, varied with the scrub or oak prairie which occupies so large a portion of the uncultivated country. At no great distance, a number of queer looking short and narrow carts, with immense wheels, attracted the attention; they formed a portion of the train from the settlements on the Red River of the North, several hundred miles distant, which had come down in about twenty-nine days, bringing furs and other commodities to exchange for supplies of provisions, etc. These carts are constructed entirely of wood, without a particle of iron; and hence their cumbrous appearance. They are commonly drawn each by one ox; but a recent improvement had substituted horses, with which they came on this trip. The remainder of the train was at Traverse des Sioux, expecting probably that the freight they wanted would be conveyed that far by the boats navigating the Minnesota River; an expectation, we thought, likely to be disappointed, if the extreme and unprecedented drought which had continued for a month should dry up the rivers much longer.

At the halfway house on this picturesque road, our friend the land hunter from Indiana alighted, the driver declining the fare he offered, for he had been some time since at service in the family of the wealthy adventurer, and regarded him as an old friend. We received a very cordial invitation to visit his family at his residence near the Northern Indiana Railroad.

Approaching the verge of the bluff which overlooks the Mississippi, the road continues in view of the river, following it upward. A distant and very imposing view of the two largest falls can be obtained, when nearing the lower town of St. Anthony. Was there ever a town, by the way, that was not divided into upper and lower? The place has but recently emerged from a wilderness into the dignity of a village, and owes its rise entirely to the lumber trade carried on, the great saw-mill near the falls, it is said, sawing several million feet of lumber during the season. In the summer months the town is much resorted to by visitors, especially from the southwestern States. These have come in such numbers that no accommodation could be found for them, and they were obliged to return with but a glance at the curiosities they had come to view. Now the state of things is more favorable to the lovers of fine scenery; an excellent hotel—the St. Charles—having recently passed into the proprietorship of Mr. J. C. Clark, and under his excellent management, already obtained a reputation as one of the best in the northwestern country. I know not where an entire summer can be passed more agreeably than at St. Anthony. In addition to beauties of scenery which have become celebrated, a wide unexplored territory opens, in which discoveries unnumbered may be made, of lakes, rivers, and cascades hitherto unknown, or of valuable lands to be had for a merely nominal price, of which the first claimant is at liberty to take undisputed possession. The region round about is, moreover, a paradise for the fisherman and huntsman.

The site of St. Anthony is a beautiful one; an

elevated plateau on the east side of the Mississippi overlooking an extent of prairie. It is about eight miles by land from St. Paul, and at high water is the head of navigation. Its advantages of water power and location will make it one day a great manufacturing place.

It is a pleasant walk or a short drive from the hotel along the river to the falls. A pond on the left of the rapid current is filled with innumerable logs, floated down the river from a distance of several hundred miles, and directed from the current into this reservoir, to be converted into boards in the saw-mill, which is in operation day and night. Above, the rapids extend half a mile—a broad wild waste of tumbling waters bordered by craggy shores, which, when the current is swollen by the spring flood, must present a sight rivalling the celebrated rapids of St. Mary's River. A little below, a foot-bridge two boards wide, shackling and uncertain, but safe enough at the present season, conducts you to an elevated, rocky island, which divides the two principal falls. This island is inhabited, and thickly wooded, and about one hundred yards wide. Crossing it at the upper end to the shore, and descending to a smooth ledge of rock, you come soon to the shelf of rock which faces the great fall of St. Anthony. This is worn by the water into a crescent form, and embraces three separate falls, besides smaller cascades. The perpendicular descent is not more than eighteen feet; but the vast body of water, the force with which it precipitates itself, the curve of the rock, and the wild beauty of the rapids above and below, together with the rush and roar of the waters, lashed into fury by their arrest among the boulders and logs heaped in wildest confusion at the foot of the descent over which they leap, throwing volumes of rainbow-crowned spray into the air, combine to impress the beholder with emotions of awe and admiration. When the river is at its greatest height, the swollen torrent descends with such impetuosity as to describe a large curve in falling, and open a cavern in the very sanctuary of the flood, where one may enter behind the falling mass, and retire so far into its recesses as to be scarcely wetted. The heaped mass of broken rocks, etc., is then overswept by the flood, or veiled by clouds of foam and spray; and the small island at the foot of the fall, which conceals the opposite fall and rapids from view, is half-buried in the rushing waters. There is no access to this island, except in winter over the frozen river. It is called "Spirit Island," from an Indian legend associated with it.

These falls are said to have been discovered about 1680 by Father Hennepin, who named them after his patron saint, St. Anthony. It is only within about thirty or thirty-five years that they have been noticed by Americans, and but recently that the number of visitors to them in a season has been considerable.

The entire descent in three-quarters of a mile has been estimated at sixty feet. Immense pieces of the rock are breaking off continually, and the falls are said to have receded several rods even since the recollection of persons who have visited them. The gorge below, with its craggy precipices, is wild and picturesque. Along its precipitous cliffs may be gathered in abundance the petrified moss, a noted product of this region, made by the dripping of limestone water from the rock below the falls.

To view the fall on the other side of the river, it is necessary to recross the foot-bridge and walk up to the larger horse-bridge; then to cross this and go down the hill to the ferry. This is another curiosity—the ferry-boat moving with its burden across the rapid water without the aid of machinery, steam or horse-power. Having reached the opposite shore, walk down the river to the old government mill on the bank, and a fine view is obtained of the tremendous rapids which form the other great fall. The grandeur of the scene grows on the sense, which becomes enlarged as you gaze upon it, to apprehend more and to be filled with a new conception of the greatness of the Creator of all this wondrous magnificence. Having feasted the eyes long upon this surpassing spectacle, you may return and recross the ferry and retrace your steps down to the precipitous bank that overlooks the Little Fall. A small division of the river is here precipitated down the rocks, but though less grand it is equally beautiful with the larger falls. Descending by a steep path, you walk along the fallen rocks, stepping from one large mass to another, till you stand within the circle of the fall, and so near that its silvery spray covers you, and you feel the rock tremble under your feet. The boulders, piled in much confusion, form numerous rifts into which the waters are driven when they plunge from above. There are two large falls; and the water of one, in its descent pitching on an upright mass of rock, falls over it in a broad sheet of foam, into the same basin that receives the descending torrent on the other side. These waters, flung together and churned into creamy foam, struggle wildly in the narrow rift, and bursting forth with tremendous impetuosity, flinging up volumes of spray, dash onward in a tortuous course to precipitate themselves down another descent, whence, joined by the smaller jets, and broken into a thousand crested waves by the fragments of rock, they move onward to the valley. The beholder must spend hours on this spot, drinking in its bewildering loveliness, before he can understand how completely the feelings may be subdued into harmony with the scene.

On the following morning an open barouche was in readiness to take us to the other interesting localities in the neighborhood. We crossed the ferry and ascending a low hill, found ourselves on an extensive prairie, a portion of the ground embraced in the military reservation of an area about ten miles square, of which Fort Snelling is near the centre. This green and softly undulating expanse was profusely covered with tall white, yellow and purple flowers, tossed by every breeze; at wide intervals stood newly framed houses ready for occupancy, but without shade or water as far as could be seen; and here and there an unfinished frame or standing boards marked a "claim" or indication that some "squatter" had selected that portion of land for his residence and intended improvements. The trenches ploughed in the soil showed the boundaries of his claim. The road is smooth and straight, requiring and receiving no mending; for the sandy soil drinks the rain without becoming the worse for it. The sloughs already alluded to as a peculiar feature in western travel, formed the exception to this rule. It was our lot on a subsequent excursion to encounter one, the stage having taken the road to the left, down to the old mill, for the purpose of affording the passengers a view of the Falls. The deceitful quagmire, covered with its green turf, was directly in the road, and the wheels going into it on the side nearest the river, we came as near an overturn as could be without accomplishing it. The sweep of landscape, varied only by the rolling of the prairie, and a tuft of trees now and then, with the distant border of forest land, offers an exhilarating view, particularly when the breeze, fresh and cool as if just from its play on the waste of waters, comes careering over it. Before the agreeable sense of novelty is over, and you have done turning from side to side to think how absolutely grand is such a prospect, the attention is suddenly arrested by a new picture. A line of blue on the edge of the horizon widens, there is a gradual sloping of the land, and in front, just below, lies the clear and beautiful sheet of Lake Calhoun.

This is said to have been named by officers of the army, some thirty-five years ago, in honor of the great statesman. It is two miles in length, and nearly circular, and with its bordering of bold shores on the other side, covered with a close garniture of woods, the gradual descent of the green prairie to its beach, and its waters clear as crystal, rippling over white pebbles, offers an irresistible temptation to linger near it. A little way down, a neat house stood on the bank; this was occupied by M. Brissette, an intelligent Frenchman, who has lived twelve or fourteen years in the vicinity. His wife is a half-breed, but speaks good French, and he has children by a former marriage, who lodged in the vicinity, having a tent pitched at hand on the green grass, in which mattresses were laid, all looking so cleanly and fresh as to give a luxurious idea of that kind of lodging. We were refreshed here by some cold water from the lake, and M. Brissette showed us a bag of cornelians and agates he had gathered from the beach, civilly inviting us to take what specimens we pleased. He keeps boats and fishing tackle for the accommodation of visitors, and his wife will set them out as good a dinner as could be wished.

A drive of two miles further brought us within view of Lake Harriet, named, tradition says, in honor of the wife of one of the officers at Fort Snelling, though certainly not of the commander's wife, for her name was Abigail. Approaching this sheet of water, which is like the other in purity and beauty, but with shores a little less elevated, we passed a strip of luxuriant bottom land, forming a small prairie. It had the much desired tall grass which grows only in moist soil, and waved like a field of standing grain as the wind swept over it. The outlet of Lake Calhoun skirts it in a rather sluggish stream, which gains impetus, however, as it nears Lake Harriet, and rushes into the latter with the force of a rapid. We drove a little way into the lake—the white sandy bottom gently sloping and smooth, and regaining the shore, followed the road around the upper end of the lake through the woods.

On the side opposite the outlet, within the shelter of the woods, were encamped the soldiers employed in cutting wood for Fort Snelling. Their tents were pitched around, and a rude open shed contained their cooking implements, and served for a kitchen. It was a comfortable picture of gipsy or pioneer life, barring the dirt and confusion of the interior of these canvass houses, so out of keeping with the fragrant herbage nature provides for their flooring, and the canopy of foliage swept by the besom of her winds and washed by rain sent from the "sweet heavens!" Since the days of our western pioneers, the more self-indulgent class of travellers have seemed to eschew this primitive shelter; "camping out" has been looked upon as a hardship rather than a luxury; and though a few adventurous young men may do it for a frolic, any women who should venture upon such an innovation could hardly fail to find themselves styled "come-outers" and "independents" in the most barbarous sense of the words. Yet if a few of them could get up sufficient self-reliance to undertake a journey through the wild parts of our country, and be content to lodge in this manner, how great would be the gain in health and pleasure!

Returning round the end of the lake, and crossing a plain thinly sprinkled with oaks, by any course that

proves most convenient, the road is regained. Through the prairie we now traverse, winds the outlet of the lakes, and is followed by the road. It is a bright swift stream, taking its way betwixt clean banks fringed with a thick growth of wild grass, variegated with flowers, and is called Little Falls Creek. It should be mentioned that this stream is the outlet of a long chain of lakes, but twelve of which have yet been explored at all. A bridge leads across it, and in a few moments it is shrouded from view by the trees on its banks. Further on we stand on the level of a bluff, and here we alighted to view one of the most beautiful of nature's works.

Parting the foliage, and descending a little way downward to a ledge of rock, you come into full view of Little Falls, or, as the Indians more poetically term it, the falls of Minne-ha-ha. In the green, shadowy depth of a wild gorge, curtained by thick woods on either hand, the swift stream above described precipitates itself in an unbroken descent of some sixty or seventy feet: the waters forming an arch of snowy foam and spray in their wild leap to the rapids below. None of the falls of Trenton are equal in beauty to this; and we viewed it with even more pleasure than those of St. Anthony.

The rock in which is set this gem of a cascade, is semicircular in form, and precipitous, dark and wild; the curve described by the falling waters leaving a cavern behind them, through which visitors can pass to the other side. The suddenness with which this vision of beauty bursts upon the sight; the contrast of the white foaming waters with the deep green of the foliage, and the dark cavern behind; the delicate streaks of light green in the falling mass; the brilliant sunshine imprisoned in its showery spray, and the rainbows dancing over it; all combine to form a scene of such enchanting loveliness as to take the senses captive, and steep the soul in the purest enjoyment this earth can afford. With a little trouble one may descend to the foot of the cascade and seat himself within reach of its diamond-like spray, listening for hours to its deep voice of music, its everlasting anthem of praise for a being which is not in vain.

The meaning of the Indian name of this exquisite waterfall is "The Laughing Waters"—and the name is well applied, for they do laugh, if not "fiercely glad," like the wild torrents of Chamouny, in the full joy of their flashing and sparkling beauty, and the ravine echoes the sound of their jubilant exultation. One should pass a day at their feet, not amid "precipitous, black, jagged rocks," whose shattered fragments tell of desolation, but in the lap of nature's most spirit-stealing nooks, where all around speaks of peace and smiling content. It is a spot where we may suppose the delicate genius of youth to have hid himself when he forsook that portion of the earth which, as the Italian poet says, "growing old, grows sad;" and here he may harbor as of yore,

"Making sunshine out of shade."

Passing on, the view opens, and from the high bluff is seen the Mississippi, with the wooded heights opposite, and a stretch of country for miles onward. The distant view of Fort Snelling, its flag gleaming in relief against the sky, is startlingly fine; but the nearer one, after a little rise, is yet more imposing. Its white walls and barracks are clearly defined, with other neat buildings in the vicinity; and all around and beyond lies spread the most magnificent panoramic display on which the eye ever rested. The Mississippi appears between its lofty bluffs, and the rich and extensive valley of the Minnesota River, seen in its serpentine course, is one of the most beautiful in the world. The village of Mendota is seen on the side opposite the fort, and the varied landscape beyond is bounded by ranges of hills rising one above another, the highest fading into the misty blue of the horizon. The view is too extensive to be embraced in a single picture to which any artist could do justice; but the eye can take it in, and will linger over it long with increasing delight.

A situation more commanding than that of Fort Snelling as seen from the Mississippi, can hardly be imagined. Its solid walls rise from the summit of nature's rampart of perpendicular rock, more than a hundred feet above the river. It stands at the junction of the Minnesota and Mississippi Rivers, and is one of the strongest military posts in the Northwest. It was begun in 1819 or 1820, and not finished for some years, having been named by Gen. Scott in honor of the commandant, Col. Snelling.

Every visitor at the Fort will be struck with the neatness and order prevailing in its interior. The buildings are substantial and elegant, and a large farm, with gardens, is attached to it, cultivated under the superintendence of the officers. Several Indians were walking about within the walls, better dressed than the generality; one or two sported cloth coats, fur hats, and military plumes, with their leggins and moccasins, while others were decked in every variety of savage finery, trinkets of silver and pewter being suspended from their ears and around their necks. They had pipes with wooden stems, four feet long, and all carried tomahawks. On the occasion of another visit, I saw some two hundred Indians who had come to receive a supply of provisions, and were assembled on the hill opposite Fort Snelling. The women and children formed a large circle on the plain, and were standing without shelter from the burning August sun to receive their share of pork and lard, which two squaws in the centre were distributing. The bags of meal or flour standing by each group showed that it had been already disposed of. It was sad to see their squalid poverty and care of this scanty allowance, which would hardly last until their return to their homes up the Minnesota. At a short distance several of the men, gayly decorated and painted, one or two appearing to be chiefs, were lying on the ground engaged in a game of cards—staking their brass bracelets and other ornaments. One sullen looking fellow wore slung on his shoulder a quiver full of beautiful arrows, barbed and curiously feathered. I drew out one to examine it, when, with a frown, he snatched it from my hand, and restored it to its place. Most of them, however, were quite willing to part with either arrows or pipes for a present in money. Crossing the ferry, and ascending the rocky hill on the other side, in a drive of four or five miles through oak openings of unrivalled beauty, we met several Indians on horseback, carrying their guns, and having bells like sleigh bells; apparently a hunting party. They stared at us with as much curiosity as we at them, and probably with impressions not more favorable. Certainly those whose ideas of the wild Indians are derived from the highly colored pictures of novelists, will risk many disappointments in seeing the reality.

Mendota is a growing place, and has been an important dépôt for the fur trade with the Indians. Skins of buffalo, elk, fox, beaver, and almost every variety, may be found here. There is a store in St. Paul for the deposit of peltry brought by the Red River trains, but we found the prices not much lower than in New-York. Indeed, but few articles of value or curiosity are brought down the rivers; most of what is offered for sale coming from below. The words "Indian curiosities," blazoned over several stores near the landings, create expectations seldom satisfied. The only rarity I was able to find, brought from Pembina, was a small bark sack, made in rude resemblance to a house, and filled with dried berries from that remote region.

The day had become very warm, or the drive back to St. Anthony would have been a charming one. The distant view of this place is remarkably fine. It shows on the elevation where it stands, like a town of much larger size. We reached the St. Charles in time to partake of a late though excellent dinner, and found some friends from Chicago.

The Dakotas gave to Carver's Cave, in Dayton's Bluff, about two miles from St. Paul, down the Mississippi, the name of Wakon Tepee—house of the spirit. It is supposed to be the place where, a century ago, the chiefs held their councils, and bones of the dead were brought from a distance to be buried on the heights above. Carver visited the cave in 1767 with some chiefs of the bands on the Minnesota River, from whom he pretended that he received a grant of the land embracing his claim to the capital of Minnesota. He describes the cave as having a tolerably wide entrance, a spacious arch within, and a lake of transparent water, a stone thrown into which produced a wonderful reverberation. He also speaks of ancient hieroglyphics cut rudely on the walls. Long since, however, all this has been changed; the roof of the cave fell in many years since, and the entrance, formerly accessible by a steep passage from the brink of the river, was closed entirely in 1820. Since then some excavations have been made, and the place now looks like a half dug cellar. In a pamphlet issued by the Minnesota Historical Society, in 1850, is a poem translated by Sir John Herschel, from the German of Schiller, entitled "Death song of a Nadowessee chief," suggested by reading a funeral address made in this cave by a Dakota chief.

Probably no country in the world more abounds in small lakes than Minnesota. Between the St. Croix and the Mississippi, they are innumerable. Their waters are crystal clear, their shores covered with sparkling pebbles, and one side is usually shaded by a dense growth of timber. Many of them have a growth of wild rice, among which are multitudes of water-fowl; and sometimes the lake opens into a swamp thickly filled with young tamaracs; the water pouring out into another reservoir, and forming another lake. Numbers are thus connected by one stream, all alive with fish and wild fowl, the game of the woods being less abundant.

I have mentioned the "claims" set up in various portions of the unsurveyed land recently ceded by the Sioux. The erection and temporary occupation of the rudest shelter, has been deemed sufficient to entitle the claimant to a pre-emption right to the portion marked out, not exceeding a quarter of a section or one hundred and sixty acres. Minnesota calls for emigrants; and with her fertile, wooded and watered territory, her advantages of navigable rivers, her sweeping prairies, her vast tracts rich in valuable timber, and her increasing lumber trade, new comers will throng to her. With the sure prospect of growing wealthy by industry and management, the settler has few or none of the privations of a pioneer to encounter; supplies can be had, and a ready market for produce, close at hand.

The Falls of St. Anthony are the point of transition from the rugged and craggy bordering of the river below to the gentle undulations of the prairie land above. There is a small steamer which ascends the Mississippi as high as Sauk Rapids, when the state of the water permits, and another to Fort Ripley; but this season it was impossible to make the trip. The stage runs once a week from St. Paul to Crow Wing, a few miles from Fort Ripley. The road, which nature herself has formed, continues from the Falls along the east bank of the river, which is in sight part of the way. The land consists of prairies, diversified with scattered groves of dwarf oak; and one is noted for a cold boiling spring in the Mississippi, which throws up gravel and pebbles with a loud noise. Though the country is not much settled, there are public houses enough on this road to provide for the comfort of travellers; and an occasional lodgment under a tent, or an impromptu supper, would be so in keeping with the wild and beautiful scene, that it could hardly be objected to. Benton County is celebrated through all the territory for its charming scenery.

Rum River is described as a deep, winding and beautiful stream, tinged with a peculiar color by the tamarac swamps through which it flows. It has its source in "Spirit Lake," or Mille Lacs, the ancient home and hunting camp of the Sioux, and its shores have been the scene of their numerous battles with the Ojibwas.

The country presents the same general character of scenery, the streams being skirted with timber, consisting of oak, maple, hickory, elm, birch, etc. Along the river shores are none of the precipitous bluffs seen below St. Anthony; the land ascends from the water in green and gradual slopes, terminating in a ridge of prairie, varied by oak openings and forests of young trees. The islands, some of which are very large, are covered with a heavy growth of elm, maple, and cottonwood, and wherever there is an abrupt elevation on the shore, it is crowned with hoary pines. The views at the mouth of Rice Creek, Swan River, and Itasca Prairie, are remarkably beautiful. At various points, fields may be seen under cultivation, affording rich promise of the excellence of the soil. An immense tamarac swamp extends along the eastern shore between St. Anthony and Sauk Rapids, designed, said a resident, "to furnish farmers with rails without splitting them." These tamarac trees, resembling a forest of tapering masts, are very picturesque in the distance. The Winnebagoes are to be seen in this region, in hunting parties, or their villages, and canoes full of them will be met, returning with supplies of provisions or goods to their homes. On the approach of the steamboat, they will glide into some little nook near the shore and wait till it has passed.

At one point the islands are so numerous and large, that they seem to arrogate possession of the channel, and the current rushes swiftly between them, giving some trouble to the boat ascending it. Buffeting the stream as it dashes down the rapids, she triumphs over the obstacles of rocks as well as sand-bars, and is presently at the destined stopping-place. At Sauk Rapids, the river spreads out over a wide expanse of granite fragments, a bar to further steamboat navigation. A row of deserted trading-houses may be seen, the Indian trade having been concentrated at Watab, a few miles further up the river. The quiet beauty of the valley between the Sauk and Watab Rivers, is not surpassed in the whole country.

The distance from St. Paul to Sauk Rapids, is about eighty miles; to the mouth of Crow Wing River, one hundred and thirty. The Indian agency was removed in 1852 from Sandy Lake to Crow Wing, Major Watrous, whom we met the year preceding at La Pointe, on Lake Superior, being the agent. The best route to this lake, we learned from traders who had frequently traversed it, is from Crow Wing up the Mississippi in canoes to Sandy Lake; thence across a portage to the St. Louis River, and down that to Fond du Lac. Voyageurs can be hired at a dollar or a dollar and a quarter per day; and for a party of three, enough to fill one large canoe, inclusive of provisions, tent, mosquito bars, &c., the expenses would be over one hundred dollars.

Surveys have been made for a road from St. Paul to Fond du Lac, and even a railroad is talked of; when that is completed, it will bring Minnesota eight or nine hundred miles nearer New-York, and open the riches of the Northwest to our citizens. A tour unrivalled for magnificence of scenery and salubrity of climate, can then be made in a few weeks from the seaboard.

The following description of Winnipeg Lake, further towards the sources of the Mississippi, is extracted from Mr. Proutwell's Journal, in the annals of the Minnesota Historical Society.

"This is a beautiful body of water, stretching from east to west fifteen or twenty miles. Here the aspect of the country again assumes a different and a pleasing character. The eastern shore is covered with a luxuriant growth of oak and maple. The trading-post is located on the northeastern shore, near the mouth of a considerable stream which empties into the lake. The land immediately about the post, is for the most part low, but of a good quality. The corn, peas, potatoes and squashes, all look well, also a small yard of tobacco. The soil is cultivated with ease. Dogs in this country, with the Canadian French, supply the place of oxen and horses, neither of which are possessed by the trader here. His house is made of logs, and, in the manner of the country, ceiled with mud. The windows are made of deer skins in their natural state, save that the hair is taken off. These, when well oiled, admit sufficient light for all the household work done here."

The "scalp-dance" witnessed at Upper Red Cedar Lake, is thus described: "Before I had returned to our tent, which is pitched but a few yards from two graves, the greater part of the Indians had collected, and begun the scalp-dance. It was led by three squaws, each bearing in her hand one of the recent scalps. Two or three men sat beating drums and singing, while old and young, male and female, all joined in the song. Occasionally all would become so animated that there would be one general leap, and all at the same time, throwing their heads back, would raise a horrid yell, clapping the mouth with the hand, to render it, if possible, more terrific. Here were seen little boys and girls, not six years old, looking on with the most intense interest, imitating their fathers and mothers, and participating in their brutal joy. At the head of the graves hung an old scalp, some ten feet above the ground, which the winds had almost divested of its ornaments and hair. The grass and the turf for several yards around, are literally destroyed, I presume, by frequent dancing. One of the scalps I examined. The flesh side had apparently been smoked and rubbed with some material till it was pliant, after which it was painted with vermilion. A piece of wood is turned in the form of a horse-shoe, into which the scalp is sewed, the threads passing round the wood, which keeps it tight. Narrow pieces of cloth and ribbons of various colors, attached to the bow, were ornamented with beads and feathers. A small stick, which serves for a handle to shake it in the air when they dance, was attached to the top of the bow by a string."

Sandy Lake has been estimated by some, to be twenty-five miles in circumference, and embraces many bays and islands. The course of the St. Louis River is through a swampy country, and extensive fields of wild rice; but in approaching Lake Superior, the land becomes more elevated, and several points command unrivalled views of scenery.

The country watered by the Crow River, is said to be equal in beauty and fertility to the valley of the Minnesota. One branch of this stream gathers its pure waters near the great bend in the Red River of the north, its southern fork draining the lakes as far west as Lacquiparle; it wanders through the "Grand Bois" of the old voyageurs, and enters the Mississippi, nearly opposite the village of Itasca. The Undine region of Nicollet, situated about the tributaries of the Mankato, or Blue Earth River, is also beautifully diversified with prairies, lakes, and forest.

The celebrated valley of the Minnesota River—called St. Pierre by the French, and until recently, St. Peter's—extends in a general direction from west to east, and, with the country along its tributaries, forms the garden spot of the territory. The principal town site in this extensive and fertile valley is Traverse des Sioux. The treaty with the upper bands was made at this place in 1851, when it presented the picturesque spectacle of hundreds of Dakota lodges, scattered along the sloping hill-side, and a concourse of Indians from remote and unexplored regions.

The mouth of the Blue Earth is about twenty miles above; and twelve miles below, at the head of the Big Woods, is La Sueur, a place which the capital and enterprise of merchants in St. Paul have already made attractive; situated on a slope rising gradually from the shore, in the midst of a fertile and lovely country. East of this, and not more than a day's drive across smooth prairies and oak groves, lies the rich valley of Cannon River, the River La Longue of La Hontan, abounding in wooded hills and picturesque lakes.

The Indian trade is chiefly carried on by the agents of large establishments, having their dépôts at St. Paul, and locating themselves at different points in the territory, and the Indian country; usually near the places where the semi-annual payments are made of annuities granted by government to the Sioux, Winnebagoes, and Chippewas. Supplies for these payments are brought up the river, and the goods furnished to the Indians by the traders, who buy furs of them, or sell at large profits on credit, in anticipation of the payments. Were I writing a description of Minnesota, many other portions of the country should be noticed; but such is not my object, and leaving the task to more competent hands, I return to our own rambles.

VIII.

WHEN has it happened, a discovery of interest, or promising useful results, being made, that some one has not been ready to observe, with an indifferent smile, "Oh, I knew of it long ago!" "It is an old story!" and the like?—so strong is the tendency, in the human nature that lusteth to envy, to refuse to industry, research and ingenuity their appropriate reward of honor. So, when it was noised abroad that a new lake, of surprising magnitude, had been found in the vicinity of St. Paul, persons here and there tossed their heads, and said, they knew those who had visited the same spot years ago; nay, that they had themselves often rode "by the place," and thought nothing strange of the enterprise, and had talked of it familiarly with the early settlers.

"Heard of it!" said an old trader to Miss C——. "Yes, to be sure I have; I can't tell for how long. Why, there's a Frenchman at 'Little Six's' village, eighty-one years old—killed duck on the wing last spring—says he has known of it ever since he can remember." This is the old man, we believe, who "has lived, for the last sixty years, within ten miles of the Falls of St. Anthony, but has never yet seen them—his business never having taken him in that direction from his home. He says he has visited nineteen different encampments in twenty-four hours, all the encampments being four miles apart or more, which would make a march on foot of at least seventy-six miles in twenty-four hours, including stoppages."

All this may be, and probably was just so. It is hardly credible that so large a body of water could exist so near Fort Snelling, and be entirely unknown or unvisited by traders, travellers, or hunters, particularly when they could derive from the Indians what information they wanted as to the remarkable localities within several days' travel. But it is undeniable that the generality of residents in the towns and settlements knew nothing of it till within a few months past. The region, belonging to the Indian, and not available to the settler, was not visited or explored, and no descriptions of its beauty of scenery had ever stimulated curiosity in regard to it. The honor of making the first exploration belongs to Mr. Simon Stevens, of St. Anthony, who, in company with Mr. C. A. Tuttle, set out in March, 1852, with a determination to find the mysterious lake of which they had heard from Indians and traders. Having ascertained its probable direction, they took their course by the compass, expecting a much longer journey than they found themselves obliged to take, for they came upon it before the day was over. Their object had been to find some suitable localities for making claims; and Mr. Stevens selected a site affording a fine water-power on the stream which forms the outlet of these lakes, and afterward conveys the waters of Lakes Calhoun and Harriet to the Mississippi. About two miles from the first lake of the chain, a rude hermit's lodge was erected, in which Mr. Stevens took up his residence.

His brother, Col. J. H. Stevens, Mr. Franklin Steele, and one or two other gentlemen, some time after set out to see the lake, which had now begun to be generally talked about, and was, by universal consent, called by its Indian name of *Minne-tonka*, or the "Big Water." A gentleman well acquainted with the Sioux language tells me the Indians call it *Mide-tonka* the "Big Lake;" but the first name has been adopted and will no doubt be retained. This party of visitors, taking with them a boat, provisions, and all conveniences for camping out, proceeded as far as Mr. Stevens's lodge, where they were hospitably entertained for the night, and the next morning went on in two boats, and explored as far as they judged it safe to venture in their small crafts on waters lashed into high waves by a strong wind. They pronounced the large lake the best fishing ground and the finest sheet of water in the territory of Minnesota.

During the summer three other parties of gentlemen went out, not with any view to exploration, but to gratify their curiosity, and amuse themselves by fishing and hunting. As there was no road, it was not deemed practicable for carriages to go, and no one unaccustomed to the endurance of hardship thought of such a thing, except in a vision of what might be a year or two hence. The idea of women going was hooted at as quite out of the question. "It is perfectly impossible!" said Judge ——; but he did not explain why, as a wagon had been out, it could not go again, or why a woman could not keep her seat in it as well as a man. This masculine selfishness in appropriating the first sights of fine scenery, and the honors of discovery with such overbearing exclusiveness, determined us on a visit to the far-famed lake.

Our anxiety to accomplish the excursion was not a little increased by the exhibition of a curious oval stone brought to St. Paul, by Dr. S., of St Louis, who had found it on the top of a promontory overlooking one of the largest lakes of the chain. It was placed upright between two sticks, painted red, and covered with small yellow spots, some of them faded to a brown color. On seeking information from a Sioux chief respecting this stone, he was told that it was regarded as sacred to the Manitou of scalps, and was visited at intervals by the warriors on their return from a battle with the scalps they had secured. These they placed as an offering on the top of the stone, which bore some rude resemblance to a human head, danced around it, and made the yellow spots to indicate the number of braves who joined in the ceremony. The scalps were always taken away, and sometimes offerings of tobacco were made; the stone being freshly painted from time to time. It had been in that same spot, the Dakota said, since his people came to the country, doubtless for generations, and had been visited within a year. The sticks supporting it were also painted.

We had been told too, that in the rocks bordering

this lake, were many bald eagles' nests, which might be reached by the hand; so little fear of man, as yet, had these monarchs of the air in this their wild and solitary home, which scarce knew the tread of the white man, or the flash of Anglo-Saxon paddles. We saw also, some eggs of a loon, a pelican, a wild goose and a wild duck, brought from the shores of this lake, and heard it variously estimated as from twenty-five to forty miles in navigable length.

When one or two resolute spirits are determined upon an undertaking, it is easy to find co-operators; and so it proved in the present instance. We drove over to St. Anthony, and there made up a party—a large wagon-load, to start the day after the morrow. On the following day I joined a pic-nic party in an excursion to Fort Snelling, and the Lakes Harriet and Calhoun, and returning in the evening was not a little chagrined to find that two of our expected company had been persuaded out of their determination by croakers, who assured them Minnetonka "was no place for ladies." They endeavored, in their turn, to dissuade us, but this was now more impossible than ever; and as luck would have it, I found M—— arranging some flowers to dry, with an agreeable English party, who had brought letters to her friend Mr. Rice, and through him been introduced to her acquaintance. "They had," as she said, "been on the Alps, been on the Apennines—admired the banks of the beautiful Rhine, and looked on the cliffs of the Upper Danube—were familiar with all objects of interest in nature or art in the British Isles, and on the continent, as well as the various phases of social and political economy abroad, and favorably disposed to acquaintance with our own society and government." The accession to our company of persons of so much taste and intelligence, desirous of enjoying to the utmost the novelty of the adventure and beauty of the scenery, was a fortunate accident.

Early on the morning of August 11th a large double wagon, light, but substantially built to withstand the inequalities of the roughest journey, was loaded with a basket of provisions supplied from the liberal larder of the St. Charles House, such light luggage as we wished to carry, and a pile of comforters, blankets and "buffaloes," as the skins are familiarly called in the country, giving rise to such amusing mistakes as occurred not long since, when a landlord, asking an English traveller if he should supply him "with two buffaloes, or would one answer,"—received the reply—"As I am not used to driving them, I will try one first." We crossed the bridge to Nicollet's island, and the ferry, and took the road over the prairie to Lake Calhoun; turning off, however, before we reached Brissette's, to the right, and passing by a rough track around the upper end of that beautiful sheet, in which the morning sun was beholding his radiant face as in the clearest of mirrors. The gentle ripple came musically up from the pebbly line of beach, and the skirting of timber stretched far away southward, forming a deep contrast to the fair blue of the watery expanse, and the sloping prairie that borders its eastern shore.

Leaving the road that bears any sign of travel, we

struck into an old Indian trail, that served rather to mark the way than to aid our progress. We skirted a broad spot of marsh or low prairie, which had once been covered with water, and now waved with tall luxuriant grass. About three quarters of a mile westward of Lake Calhoun, we came upon another small, circular lake, equally clear and beautiful, to which the Indians long ago gave a name, signifying "The Lake of the Isle of Red Cedars." We saw no cedars any where; but it is a lovely sheet, and famous for the capture of a two horse wagon load of fish by a couple of sportsmen. Hereabouts we found the frame of a neat log cabin—that is, the logs *unchinked*—standing; probably built by some claimant who intends to take possession as a resident. The country we passed through was chiefly what is called burr or scrub oak openings, sprinkled with stunted trees, and thickly covered with a growth of hazel, wild cherry bushes, etc., to the height of two or three feet. This was varied by patches of closer woodland in which the birch and maple, as well as the oak, were seen, while far to the right were groves of tamarac and large timber. Meadows of marsh grass of small or great extent, brilliant in their light green vesture, were bordered by ranges of upland. They had evidently once been lakes. The elevated ground rose rather abruptly from these bottom lands, and it was necessary to follow the ridge, which sometimes became so narrow as scarcely to afford room for the passage. The faintest trace of a road had now disappeared, and our course through the trackless wild was taken by the compass—our guide, moreover, who had brought out the other parties, being familiar with it. At every step forward we laid prostrate the young oaks and luxuriant bushes, now climbing a pitch so steep it seemed almost perpendicular—now descending one where the wagon appeared fated to fall and crush our faithful horses; or winding along the edge of a declivity, in a position so sideling it seemed impossible to sustain a foothold—knowing nothing, withal, of what was to come, or through what perils we should issue safely. We proceeded for several miles at a very slow pace, and the beauty of the landscape called forth continual exclamations. "Stained strawberry leaves, and the more brilliant red of the sumach, the sombre yellow of the hazel, and the fading green of the Cornus tribes, mingling with the bright glossy hue of the oak, made a picture it is not strange painters have failed to imitate."

Setting aside the roughnesses of the way, one might find it difficult to believe he had passed beyond the limits of civilization. Sometimes the ridge we followed passed between two crystal lakelets, or low meadows of vivid green, and the foliage around us was of every shade of verdure. It looked not at all like a primeval forest; but we had learned to be familiar with the knowledge that we were treading ground to which the white man's claim had never reached as yet—over which the Indian had held sway from a period beyond the memory of tradition. Now and then we came upon an old camping ground where was still visible the trace of their fires, and where the poles over which the Sioux lodges are built were still standing. These were always on smooth grassy plains—for the time is past when the covert of woods was necessary to protect the savage from lurking enemies. Passing over a beautiful rolling prairie, bordered with a distant line of forest, and sprinkled with tufts of trees like islets, it had such an appearance of cultivation that we looked involuntarily for the reapers of this magnificent field, and a white cottage to peep out behind the cluster of foliage. Again, a stately park of oaks, with its broad, shaded avenues, and lake set like a gem in the midst of embowering foliage, seemed to belong of right to some proud mansion appropriate to so rich a domain. There was appearance of wild plums, crab-apples, grapes, and other indigenous fruits, with strawberries, blackberries, and cranberries in their season.

Our guide pointed out, afar off, an oval-shaped mound, said to be three hundred feet high, and to command an extensive view of the country for miles around. Towards that hill our course was to be directed, and in all turnings and windings, we never lost sight of it. Then we entered a dense wood of heavier timber than we had seen, an overarching wood, that shut out the sunshine, leaving only room enough for our narrow vehicle to pass; the meeting branches having to be parted as we went on, and occasionally giving us a smart tap or thrust, as if the genius of the place were determined to resent our invasion of his wild solitude. The intolerable heat made the woods a pleasant shelter, and we cared less for the steep hills we had to ascend and descend. Still on we went, skirting marshes and climbing ridges as before, our courage in no way diminished, till three or four miles beyond a small lake, the welcome sight of a broad bright stream, rushing along with current "fiercely glad," made us aware that we approached the termination of our drive. We could see it afar, winding and flashing through the meadow, and the clustering bushes bent low to dip their branches in its clear, deep waters. "Little Falls Creek," said our guide, in answer to our question, what was its name; and we recognized the same lovely stream we had marvelled at on our way to Fort Snelling, and in its bewitching leap at the falls of Minnehaha. We forded this rapid outlet, ascended to the summit of a ridge dividing two lakelets, ploughed our way through a forest of undergrowth along the margin of a broad meadow, and came into full view of—a haystack!

This was an unwelcome sight to a party anxious to escape from all sign or token of "the settlements;" but we were presently consoled on being informed it was "the hermit's hay." Poor recluse! we might, without detriment to the most fastidious romance, allow him the privilege of cutting and drying the wild grass—to serve for a couch, perhaps, or the like; for we had ascertained, to our entire satisfaction, that he kept no stock of any kind. We should, however, have preferred seeing a man dressed in skins, or even wrapped in an Indian blanket, answer the loud call of our driver, to the sight of one robed in common farmer's fashion when at work, with ruddy, cheerful countenance, in which good humor and content were so evident as to preclude the very shadow of melancholy.

This was not the hermit—who chanced to be absent from home—but Mr. S——, one of his friends, who occasionally assisted him in his clearing and other labors. Our guide called to him—then went in search of him; he came up on the other side, meanwhile, and welcomed us with much courtesy, apologizing for the homeliness of the accommodation he had to offer, and intimating slightly a wish that we had delayed our visit till "things had been got a little nicer—a house built, and so forth." We assured him the wildness of the scene was its principal charm in our eyes, and then turned to look for our Jehu, who had disappeared in the search after Mr. S——. When he returned and took his seat, we proceeded by the roughest way we had yet gone over, and made several doublings and descents before we reached the lodge.

This stood on a wide peninsula formed by a bend in the stream, which just below rushes down a considerable fall, forming a beautiful rapid, and giving the value of a fine water-power to the locality. On the other side of the creek to the left, rose a range of conical hills of moderate elevation; on the right, the sloping uplands stretched away, inclosing a broad plain of meadow land. The ground every where was very thinly sprinkled with dwarfed oaks, with here and there a pine or cedar, to the distant border of close woods, but the undergrowth was thick where it had not been burnt over. The lodge was as unpoetical a shelter as could well be imagined. It was built of rough boards, with pretty wide crevices between; was low and small, and unprotected from the burning sun by the least shade; a well beaten path on either side led through the bushes to the stream, and another, not so marked, to a spring at some distance.

The door was hospitably thrown open, and we looked within. About one third of the space was occupied by a mosquito bar stretched over a bed on the floor, if bed it might be called, which was only a shake-down of straw covered with a blanket. In the opposite corner stood a large cooking-stove, and a couple of shelves, the lower one of which served as a dresser, and held sundry pans, platters, and tin vessels. Heavier cooking utensils were ranged below, with a washing tub and two or three wooden pails. The only toilet conveniences were a tin wash basin, and a small cased looking-glass suspended from the upper shelf, with two or three coarse but clean towels hanging near it. A small and roughly constructed table stood on the side nearest the door, and beside it the jug, which usually contained spring water. The platters and cooking implements were clean, but the floor seemed guiltless of scouring, and notwithstanding the heat of the sun and want of shade trees, we found it more agreeable to stay without till the gentlemen had the boat ready.

The basket was unpacked, meanwhile, and a hasty lunch taken, for we had several miles further to go, and it might be late before our return. Those who were bent on fishing made their preparations, and leaving our luggage in the wagon, and fastening the horses, we took the footpath to the landing-place, just on the bend of the stream. Some young frogs were taken for bait among the weeds on the margin, and presently the whole party was seated in the boat, paddling up the deep, swift outlet.

The water is from two to six feet or more deep, and would serve for steamboat navigation. A small steamer was talked of for another season, and a mill, for which Mr. Stevens was then hauling lumber. It was slow work paddling up the current with so many passengers, through the serpentine windings of the creek. Its banks were fringed with willows and bushes, with here and there a clump of trees so tastefully disposed, that a landscape gardener would have been enchanted. The waters were so clear we could often see the sandy bottom, and numbers of fish sporting round us; they had not yet learned to dread the angler! The white and yellow lilies grew profusely near the banks, which were now marshy, now rising to an elevated ridge of oakland. Then we entered the woods, and the uplands rose into hills of considerable elevation, covered densely with foliage; a long peninsula was rounded, and about four miles from the shanty we found ourselves in a clear and beautiful lake, the first in the chain we were entering. This bright sheet, the eastern arm of Minnetonka, was nearly circular, and a mile across in any direction. As we shot over its unruffled surface, we asked each other what name should be given to this first brilliant in the garland of gems; and claiming the right, as the first white women who had ever looked on its beauty, to bestow a name, in compliment to the English portion of our party we called it Lake Browning—after the great poetess.

Some have objected to the giving of separate names to the different divisions of this extensive body of water, parted as they are merely by peninsulas, with channels devoid of current. But for the sake of convenience they will in time receive names, and it is well to save them from some inharmonious cognomen, connected perhaps with no agreeable associations. Portions of this lake, near the shores, are covered with wild rice, rushes, and water lilies, and the shrill, plaintive cry of the loon might be heard at short intervals.

Passing through a narrow strait, we then entered the second lake, rounding a sharp point, and started with surprise at the picture which unexpectedly presented itself. A noble sheet of water, nearly three miles in width, and three and a half long, lay embraced by lofty bluffs, not rocky, but rising almost perpendicularly from the pebbly shores, densely wooded nearly to the water's edge, and having their ridges and summits covered with tall, heavy timber. Some distance back of these extends a fine prairie. Two bold headlands, about midway up, stretched far out into the lake, and at our left the loveliest cove in the world, with a beach of white sand and pebbles, was pointed out as a splendid fishing ground. Two of the gentlemen landed here with all necessary apparatus for making havoc among the finny tribes. But first, with due formality, and reverently standing, we gave to the lake the name I had chosen—Lake Bryant—and read aloud a few lines from the poet appropriate to the scene:

"Still this great solitude is quick with life;
Myriads of insects, gaudy as the flowers

They flutter over; gentle quadrupeds,
And birds that scarce have learned the fear of man,
Are here; and sliding reptiles of the ground,
Startlingly beautiful. The graceful deer
Bounds to the woods at my approach; the bee,
A more adventurous colonist than man,
With whom he came across the eastern deep,
Fills the savannas with his murmurings,
And hides his sweets, as in the golden age,
Within the hollow oak. I listen long
To his domestic hum, and think I hear
The sound of that advancing multitude
Which soon shall fill these deserts."

It was on this lake that a deer was speared in the water by the first party of visitors, while the creature was swimming across. Deer and other game abound, it is said, in these woods, and wild birds that build on inaccessible heights, have their nests in the boughs of these lofty cedars. We saw one noble eagle poised on the wing over our heads, and looking down as if in wonder at our invasion of his home. A gentleman who was there in the spring, told me he had climbed a tree to rob an eagle's nest, but had been fiercely attacked by the parent bird. On the beach, agates and cornelians may be picked up in abundance, and one of fine quality which I brought away will make, when cut, a beautiful memorial of the locality.

An extremely narrow isthmus connects Lake Bryant with the third lake. We landed and climbed, over ragged prominences and fallen cedars, the steep promontory dividing their waters, and having gained a height of some sixty feet, gazed upon the scene before us with emotions of wonder and admiration. The lofty headland is half a mile in length, running out from the southern shore of the lake, and for some distance from the point is not more than two rods in width. Its prevailing growth is red cedar, with a tangled undergrowth which has shot up between the decaying limbs of the dead trees, fallen, perhaps, centuries ago. The signs of Dakota worship show indubitably that the place was holy ground. Here, says a writer in the Minnesotian—"the heathen orgies of a great and powerful race, for whose ancient homes we have just bartered a pittance of our trashy gold, were celebrated long before the world-seeking Genoese reared the flaunting standard of Castile and Aragon upon the shores of the Haytian seas. The appearance of the ground; the marks upon the trees; the ruins of rude altars; remnants of old scalp hoops; the painted stone, and all such implements of savage rites, prove this theory correct." It was from this spot that the sacred boulder above mentioned was taken. The name proposed for it is Point Wakon,* and thus let it be.

The view from this point up the lake was a magnificent one, partaking of grandeur in no slight degree; for the fresh breeze, which had not full play on the other lakes, here lifted the waves into billows and flung them on the beach at our feet with a surgelike murmur. Far as the eye could reach stretched the blue, sparkling waters, sprinkled here and there with islands thickly wooded, and bordered with a deep, dark forest, wholly unlike the woods on the uplands,

* The Dakota term for any thing spiritual or supernatural.

for the trees were of great height and size. Col. Stevens informed us he had hereabouts seen the white oak measuring sixty feet from the ground to its branches. The timber was chiefly of oak and elm of different kinds; the white oak, sugar maple, hickory, poplar, cotton wood, etc., with a few evergreens. Long and narrow peninsulas from either shore, rising into promontories of startling abruptness and height, projected miles into the lake, some not more than twenty feet wide, forming beautiful bays, in which, they say, fish are in marvellous abundance. Two small islands lay just before us, tufted with thick green foliage, and midway up the lake, a large and beautiful one, embracing, it is said, a thousand acres; a place resorted to by the Indians for making sugar. The greatest width of this lake is estimated at over ten miles; its length from Point Wakon to the point of connection with the fourth lake, rather less. It has a branch lake stretching northward, from the west extremity of which to Point Wakon it is several miles. This branch sheet, which is not reckoned in the chain, is said to have formed the division in former times between the assembled forces of the Sioux and Chippewas, when they came for the purpose of deadly strife, and encamped on either side. The fourth lake is the largest in the chain, and bears, by way of special distinction, the name Minnetonka, by which the whole range is called. It is said to have the finest scenery, and to be walled by rocky, precipitous cliffs, towering to a considerable height; but we could not have judged of this without sailing a number of miles, past the headlands whose blue outline formed the limit of our view. This fourth lake has also a branch lying northward, and is said to contain ten islands of considerable size. A narrow stream connects it with a fifth and much smaller lake, and westward of this the others follow in succession. Col. Stevens said the number in the chain was sixteen, as he had ascertained by actual exploration, and that the last lake approached within a very few miles of Minnesota River. The whole range runs nearly east and west. Mr. S., who accompanied us, informed me that in the beginning of this month, he and a friend had found canoes in a cove beyond the farthest point in the third lake, and a well marked Indian trail leading westward. They followed the trail, starting at seven in the morning, and after a walk of a few hours arrived at "Little Six," a Sioux village on the Minnesota. Dining there, they returned in the afternoon to the lake. The features of the country back of the timbered strip of land were oak openings and rolling prairies. On the shore of this third lake a location has been chosen, and claims set up for a hundred families who are to remove thither next year. In some remote places we saw them designated by mere slips of board nailed against a tree.

We felt no surprise to hear that this charming region had been so valued by the Dakotas as a hunting and fishing ground, that they were said to have kept the knowledge of it from the white population as long as possible, and petitioned the Governor for a reservation of territory which would have included this favorite possession. They loved this beautiful land, its clear water and deep forests; their ancient hunting-ground, and the scene of their battles and sacrifices. There is reason, indeed, to suppose that they came yearly to make offerings to their deities hereabouts. But the rapacity of the white man denied them this beloved retreat, and emigrants already press in to occupy the country of the receding race. A year or two more will banish their canoes from these waters, and show the majestic headlands sprinkled with clearings and germs of settlements. Even now preparations are making for the erection of a hotel near Lake Browning, and the construction of a road to St. Anthony, in anticipation of the hunting and fishing parties expected the ensuing season from all parts of the United States.

One of the promontories was described by a visitor who came after us, as abounding in groves of sugar-maple, one tree measuring three feet in diameter. The white oak, hickory, ash, basswood, etc., vary the growth, and the soil would be favorable to wheat crops. We landed at the foot of a steep promontory in Lake Bryant, and climbing it, plunged into the deep and cool recesses of a stately wood, reminding us of the dense forests of the eastern States.

On our way back we took up our anglers with their string of fish, and reached the hermit's landing about dusk, somewhat weary, but rejoicing for the beauty we had seen. Then came the less agreeable part of the romance of camping out. Mr. S. made a fire in the cooking stove which occupied so large a space in the cabin, while others kindled brushwood outside, and covered the fire with leaves and turf—making what is called in Western parlance, a "smudge"—the smoke of which was intended to keep off mosquitoes. The table was set in the open air, and in due time the party sat down to supper, the smoking fish, fried pork and bread and butter having a relish they never could have possessed under other circumstances. The serious business of clearing the table and washing the dishes was postponed till daylight, for the smudge was dying away for want of fuel; we could not consent to have any of the sparsely scattered trees felled—and the mosquitoes began to make desperate sallies. Then came repentance for our want of thought in not bringing tents. The shanty offered shelter for the women, but the five gentlemen were obliged to sleep wrapped in buffalo skins, with only the sky for a roof, and exposed to the merciless hordes of our insect foes, which having deserted the inhabited parts of Minnesota, seemed the more bent on revenging the intrusion into their wilderness domain. Having secured the cabin door, and placed two carriage cushions for pillows, we crept under the netting and lay down on the floor pallet; but no fatigue could bring me repose. The heat, and the fumes of cookery; the gambols of a number of field mice which had got in through the crevices, and were feasting on the remnants of our repast, with the fear that the little creatures might next pay us a visit, were sufficient to banish slumber; the horses, too,—our faithful companions from St. Anthony, were tied just outside;

their noses rubbed against the boards, and they discussed the hay furnished them, with very audible chewing, to a period quite within "the short, small chimes of day," occasionally varying the performance by switching off mosquitoes with great vigor, lashing the partition to the imminent danger of cheeks close to it, or beating violently against it with their hoofs. Now and then, with a desperate leap, they would spring from the ground, and there remained no doubt on my mind that they had broken their fastenings, and were setting out on their homeward journey, leaving us to follow as we best might. So wore away the night, and as the day began to break, a movement of our friends without, and the gathering of fishing tackle, showed they were bent on some early sport. It seemed but an instant after, when a curious *fizzing* roused me, and the bass they had caught might be seen in the pan, frying under the auspices of Miss C—, who showed an admirable knowledge of culinary mysteries on this occasion. In the mean time Mr. S. had arranged the breakfast table on the green, in perfect order, fetched a bucket of cool spring water, and was diligently slicing up a loaf of bread. A walk to the creek disclosed the place for morning ablutions, where willow boughs drooped lovingly over the clear deep water, and presently we were seated around the simple board, the bright sun shining upon us, and illuminating a lovely landscape, not the less admired because the hand of man had never sought to embellish it. When the meal was over, the horses were put to the wagon, the luggage repacked, and having bade adieu to our courteous host, we returned to St. Anthony, following, as nearly as possible, the trail we had made in coming. On one of the elevations we crossed within four or five miles, was found the wild sage, mentioned as growing so extensively on the plains of Oregon and California. From the highest peak of this region, it is said, a view can be had of a large part of Minnetonka, of the Minnesota and Mississippi rivers, and the distant town of St. Anthony.

IX.

THAT portion of Minnesota Territory which lies along the St. Croix River, though one of the earliest explored, and the best for farming purposes, has not become well known. The regions directly adjacent to the Mississippi have naturally received more attention, and the course of travel and emigration has been chiefly up the valleys of the Mississippi and Minnesota rivers. Various local publications, too, have set forth the advantages of these, while the eastern branches have been comparatively neglected, or left to the slower diffusion of knowledge gained by actual settlers. Yet there is no section presenting more attractions to both the farmer and the merchant than the valley of St. Croix. The Falls of St. Croix—thirty miles above Stillwater, and sixty from the mouth of the Lake, is the furthest north of any navigable point from the Mississippi.

A regular stage runs from St. Paul to Stillwater, the road passing over extensive tracts of upland prairie, and through oak openings like fruit orchards. About fifteen small lakes are seen, and several rapid streams. The drought had prevented any boats of large size going up the St. Croix for many weeks, and it was with surprise that we heard, on entering St. Paul one morning, that the "Black Hawk" on her return from Traverse des Sioux, had been chartered to take freight up that river, and was to start in a few moments. It was four in the afternoon when the steamer was ploughing her way down the Mississippi to Point Douglas, situated at the junction of the two rivers. Upon the tongue of land extending between is "Cottage Grove," a fertile spot, where farmers raise produce to send up to market. The thriving settlers in the neighborhood are from Maine. After leaving the Mississippi, we entered through a narrow channel into Lake St. Croix. The difference between its clear, smooth waters, and the river surface vexed with currents, is instantly perceptible. Bluffs line the shore on the left hand; on the other is a low wall of rocks, gradually rising and receding a little as you advance, till they too become towering heights. The graceful curve of the line of shore, the alternate swelling and sinking of the wooded hills, the deep ravines occasionally opening between them—the dark shadows thrown by the heights on the water, with the narrow line of light near the shore marking the departure of the sun, and now and then a projecting headland further out, a dark and shaggy mass—were so beautiful, that one could not regret the scenery of the Mississippi. The lake varies from half a mile to two or three miles in width, and along its banks at intervals are seen farm houses, and the log cabins of recent settlers.

Willow River, a small village within six miles of the head of the lake, was passed and the boat stopped for the night at Stillwater. This town, settled some eight or ten years, stands at the head of the lake, and is the great mart for lumber of the St. Croix, commanding an extensive and rich farming country. It is picturesquely situated at the foot of a circular range of hills, at the lower end of which the heights become precipitous, and are capped with turret-like masses of rock fifteen or twenty feet in depth, extending around the whole summit of the bluff, and presenting the appearance of architectural ruins. The dwelling-houses are sprinkled along the sides of the declivity as well as on the plain, and some are built on very elevated ground. The Court-House stands on the brow of the hill. A fine spring on the hill side, the water collected in a large reservoir, fenced with a high stone wall, supplies water to a large part of the town. I counted three public houses from one point of view: the Stillwater House, the Minnesota House, and the Lake House, which stands close to the water. A very neat church is seen from the lake, and there are others. A new Penitentiary is building, which makes some stir among laboring men, and brings money into the place. It stands in a fine situation on the river, half a mile above the town, in what is called "Battle Hollow," a battle having been fought there some ten years since between the Sioux and Chippewas.

There are two mills of two saws each, one driven by steam and one by water power; one was nearly buried by the sand washed from the bluff, but will soon be again in operation. The prospects of the town are flourishing, and its advantages of location and the natural resources of the country must soon make it a place of importance and wealth.

St. Croix River was so named after a Frenchman, who found a grave in its waters. Above Stillwater it flows between high bluffs, with occasionally an opening by which easy access is had to the interior. The woods are dense, and extend back, consisting of oak, ash, elm, basswood, and great quantities of maple. The gleaming of sunrise on the rounded masses of foliage stretching out into the lake at its upper extremity, lofty bulwarks that stand as if to guard the pass, and on the high northward range, could not be rivalled by the artist's pencil. "Paint Rock" forms a picture that might be a study for a landscape painter. The cliffs rise perpendicularly from the water, to the height of thirty or forty feet, sometimes overhanging the river so as to form deep cavernous openings. The rock is formed of layers variously and richly colored. Above the solid rampart tower the hills, partially covered with tall trees, and wearing their shaggy crown. This is a locality held in veneration by the Sioux, and numerous pictures and hieroglyphics are said to be carved and painted on the perpendicular wall. Several Ojibwas were here killed by the Sioux some years since. On the Wisconsin side, as you ascend, the sheer wall rises to the height of sixty feet or more, lifting itself perpendicularly from the narrow line of shore. The gorgeously colored stone contrasts with the deep green of the woods at its base, and ragged evergreens on the summit stand in relief against the sky. Islands fringed with willows dot the river here and there, where the wild grass waves in the greatest luxuriance.

Still ascending, you find the same lofty rampart, craggy at its base and summit, with a belt of dense foliage, except where the face of the cliff is entirely covered with broken masses of rock. The eye rests with pleased attention on a conical height on the Minnesota side, whose castellated summit presents the appearance of hoary ruins, the opposite side being a cavernous, savage looking range of rocks, rendered wilder in appearance by stunted trees growing in their rifts. The stream is now closely embraced between these barriers, now expands to greater width to inclose its wooded islands. No more exquisite landscape could be pictured by fancy than the one seen at this point in looking back. The headlands on either side approach near each other, the morning sunshine is golden on their woods; the calm water lies like a sheet of silver between, and the background is a lofty forest-covered bluff. In the foreground is an island covered with tall trees, the only undergrowth being the tall grass, brilliantly green. A succession of such pictures, each as it seems, more lovely than the other, is offered as we continue to ascend—varied only by the different height and position of the hills, and the islands slumbering on the dark, smooth waters.

A little further up the river the shores become less elevated, the hills receding—and strips of bottom land stretch out, terminated at some distance back by the higher ridges. The timber is much larger and denser than on many of the bottoms of the Mississippi. It is not long, however, before the same bluffs appear. At short intervals clear springs gush up from their foot, and send out their tribute in sparkling rills that hasten to the river. It is said there are great numbers of speckled trout in these mountain streamlets.

A house appears now and then, the germ of a settlement, and it is curious to note how picturesque are these pioneer habitations, perched among the woods, and how readily the advance of improvement defaces the romance of the view. The settler spares not the leafy honors of the forest, for to him a potato patch has more charms than a grove. Occasionally the standing poles of Dakota lodges may be seen. "Marine Mill" on the eastern side of the river, is twelve miles above Stillwater, and occupies a site formed by nature for a town, in the mouth of a beautiful gorge. Some of the houses are extremely neat, and have cultivated gardens; they stand on a table-land, on the top of an inconsiderable elevation, and two or three miles back is to be found some of the best farming land in the territory. In the vicinity is a Swedish settlement, of an intelligent and industrious population. The Marine Mill Company is said to be wealthy and enterprising; they have partly finished a new mill, to supersede the the old one, which has been in use twelve or fifteen years.

The country between Stillwater and Marine is described as being broken, and of varied soil and aspect, exhibiting the usual alternations of rolling prairie and groves of oak, with some large timber. Cornelian

Lake, further down, is noted for the beautiful pebbles found on its shores, and we were told that a pretty waterfall is to be seen in the vicinity of the place.

At this landing we had an accession of agreeable lady passengers, Mrs. Hall, the wife of our good captain, having been hitherto our sole companion. I have forborne to describe the terrible sandbars which, since the long continuance of high water, had partly filled up the channel. We struck on them a dozen times, each involving a delay of several hours. In such cases it was necessary to send out a boat with men and ropes, tie a rope round some stout tree, and haul the boat over; or, if that would not do, to lighten the freight by removing some of it into barges alongside. The slow working over a formidable bar, when one's time is precious, is about as severe a test of patience as could well be devised. It is one of the prominent features of western steamboat travelling, and frequently lengthens into days a journey performed in a few hours at high water. Now and then "all hands" had to leap ashore and cut down wood from the bottoms to feed the engine, while the boat thus labored along.

Another fine subject for a landscape painter is afforded about twelve miles below the Falls. The bluffs on the Minnesota side rise to a commanding height, approaching nearer the river; a circular island lies directly in the foreground, so densely covered with tall trees that the sunshine cannot enter, and fringed thickly with waving grass; the course of the river is seen above, following the curve of the heights, and their impervious drapery of woods presents every variety of shades in green, mingled with the darker hue of spirelike evergreens. A little below are the large "standing cedars," which form the boundary line between the Sioux and the Chippewa nations. The height of the bluffs and boldness of the whole shore, with the gently winding course of the stream, and its numerous islands, afford picturesque points at every turn. There is a large lime-kiln further up, and the woods bordering the river are dense and dark. At the bend a little below the small settlement they call Osceola, there is a beautiful grove of the white pine, a variety in the rich masses of summer foliage.

Rock Island rises abruptly from the bed of the river with its encircling belt of rock, and on either side the perpendicular cliffs of trap-rock rise to the height of fifty or sixty feet, brilliantly and variously colored as before—their perfect reflection in the clear mirror of the stream giving a finer effect to the picture.

Within a short distance of the termination of our voyage, a scene presented itself which nothing on the Upper Mississippi can parallel. The stream enters a wild, narrow gorge, so deep and dark, that the declining sun is quite shut out; perpendicular walls of trap-rock, scarlet and chocolate-colored, and gray with the moss of centuries, rising from the water, are piled in savage grandeur on either side, to a height of from one hundred to two hundred feet above our heads, their craggy summits thinly covered with tall cedars and pines, which stand upright at intervals on their sides, adding to the wild and picturesque effect; the river, hemmed in and overhung by the rocky masses, rushes impetuously downward, and roars in the caverns and rifts worn by the action of the chafed waters. These sheer and awful precipices, mirrored in the waters, are here broken into massive fragments, there stand in architectural regularity, like vast columns reared by art; or some gigantic buttress uplifts itself in front of the cliffs, like a ruined tower of primeval days. One slender shaft, a solitary pillar, is seen ; the top formed like a chair, in which an eagle might build its nest. A high and hoary cliff in front, seeming to bar further progress, appears the end of the river. But a sharp turn to the left discloses the rapids; just before us stand two solid enormous masses of rock like the abutments of a bridge and a notch between them is the landing-place, a long bridge of boards conducting from the bow of the boat to the land.

We had but little time, after so many delays, to walk up stream a mile or so, for a view of the main rapids that give this place the name of the Falls of St. Croix. There is a succession of rapids, with swift water intervening, for six or seven miles, the entire fall estimated at about seventy-five feet, and the main rapids having a descent of twenty feet in as many rods. It is only here that a portage would be necessary with bateaux, though at points above, skill is required on the part of the boatmen. For nearly a mile up, the bank is composed of masses of rock from thirty to fifty feet high. A broad strip of table-land, with soil of black loam, extends to the foot of the higher bluffs.

Descending the rocks to the bed of the river, the narrowed stream can be seen rushing wildly over ledges of rock. Climbing to the level of the table-land, and walking to the point, a boulder on its verge commands a very fine view of the rapids higher up, and the winding river above.

The village of St. Croix Falls is on the Wisconsin side opposite the main rapids, and its beauty of situation and local advantages, should have made it by this time a populous town. The first claim was made here in the summer of 1839, soon after the ratification of the Chippewa treaty, by a company from Illinois, of whom were William S. Hungerford, the present proprietor, and Franklin Steele, the principal owner of the mills at St. Anthony. They erected a large saw-mill, boarding-house, shops for mechanics' labor, etc, and commenced operations. Within a few years the property had passed into other hands, and by the several conveyances and the death of one of the owners, the title had been brought in dispute. The great advantages of the location attracting attention, other negotiations were then opened, a joint-stock company was formed, part of the purchase money paid down, and a plan organized for the building of a city which might become the seat of government for a new Territory; for the northern boundary of Wisconsin, at that time unsettled, was expected to be further south. Men of wealth and political influence were interested in carrying out the design, and in the spring of 1847 operations were commenced under the most promising auspices. Large store-houses, etc. were built, and a spacious hotel was nearly completed. But the Mexican war drew two chief members of the company from the embryo capital, and the conditions of the contract not having been fulfilled, Mr. Hungerford placed an injunction on the further proceedings of the company. Since that time a tangled lawsuit has prevented their progress, the property being held sometimes by one party—sometimes by the other, and pending these difficulties the buildings have fallen into decay, and no further improvements have been made. The basement of the great hotel is a summer resort for cattle as a shelter from the sun. The saw-mill has been kept in operation during the summers, by a lease under whichever party—"the Boston Company," or the "Injunction party"—chanced, by decree of court, to have temporary possession; but the liability to be dispossessed, and the want of capital to manage independently so heavy a business, or secure payment to the workmen by the employers, have had the usual consequences, disastrous to enterprise, and accidents have rendered thorough repairs necessary. When in good order the mill is capable of cutting from five to six million feet of lumber during the season of seven months and a half, and affords employment to more than fifty men. The common price of sawing is four dollars a thousand, and a workman's wages amount to nearly forty dollars a month, including board. Supposing the gross yearly income to be twenty thousand dollars, and the expense of labor in sawing nine thousand, the operator should realize a handsome nett profit out of the remaining eleven thousand, after paying the cost of repairs, etc.

Thirty or forty rods below the mill is a beautiful cascade, and at intervals between this and the steamboat landing are large springs, which would afford ample water-power for many kinds of machinery. At the landing near the foot of the rapids, the steamboat freight is deposited, and thence taken in bateaux to St. Croix Falls. The river is compressed into a narrow compass called the Dells, the water, when high, rushing through with great force. Just above this a dam might be built, affording a fall of eight or ten feet. "Taylor's Falls" is the county seat and central point for business of Chisago county, which was organized in January 1852. The first claim was made in 1839 by Jesse Taylor, of Stillwater, after whom the place was named, and improvements were commenced under the auspices of a company, nearly at the same time as at St. Croix Falls; but no great progress was made before Mr. Folsom's purchase of an interest in the property, in the fall of 1850. In the following spring the town was surveyed and laid off into village lots. It now contains two store-houses, two stores, two taverns, one law office, one blacksmith shop, one mill for grinding corn, and several dwellings. The old log store-house built by the first claimants is yet standing, having served in its turn for store-house, store, tavern, post-office, dwelling-house, carpenter's shop, school-house, ball-room and church, besides being supposed to be haunted by ghosts.

From the summit of a high hill on the Wisconsin side, three small lakes may be seen. The country in the immediate neighborhood is broken and rocky, and not of inviting appearance. The river below the rapids is hid by the curve in the stream, and the intervening wild bluffs. The table-land extends nearly a mile up stream, and is bounded by a bluff seventy or eighty feet high, back of which stretches a beautiful level tract to the foot of a more elevated trap rock ridge.

Taylor's Falls, as already mentioned, is the most northerly point of continuous navigation on the Mississippi or any of its tributaries, and the natural dépôt for lumber from the vast region of the pineries. At a common stage of water, the boats running above Galena can ascend to this place; at other times freight is brought up in bateaux. In the latter part of the season of 1852, a small "seven by nine" boat, called "Queen of the Yellow Banks," plied between the Falls and Stillwater, and did a brisk business; but a boat running only to Stillwater does not meet the public want, the freight being shipped at St. Louis, Galena, and intermediate points. Six miles above, at the head of the rapids, two or three farms have been opened. From this point, in going up the St. Croix, we find it little diminished below the mouth of Snake River; a steamboat of light draft could thus run fifty or sixty miles, and probably further during high water. The boats used at present are bateaux of about eighteen hundred weight, poled by two boatmen. The prospects opening for the country render it inevitable that the farmers shall grow rich; new settlers are wanted and invited, and notwithstanding the setting *westward* of the steady current of emigration, they must soon begin to fill the country.

A band of Chippewas formerly had their headquarters at the Falls. They have now disappeared, the few who remain being very indolent, and living by hunting, begging and stealing. Their favorite haunt is the grog shop, and in past years several traders have been killed by them. In the spring of 1848 two white men were found murdered about six miles east of the Falls. An Indian was arrested, tried, and found guilty of the murder, and immediately hung. Before ascending the scaffold, which consisted of two barrels, one standing on another, under the limb of a large oak tree from which the rope was suspended,—he called for a pipe, and sat down and smoked with the stoical indifference characteristic of his race. A white man suspected of having incited the Indian to the deed, was tied to the tree, severely whipped, and told that his life would no longer be secure if he did not leave the country within twenty-four hours. Such proceedings were considered necessary in the exposed situation of these frontier settlements surrounded by savages, and separated by a wide tract of wilderness from civilized communities.

We had cherished the hope of being able, even with our small party, to cross from the Falls of St. Croix to La Pointe, and terminate our summer excursion by descending Lake Superior. A professed voyageur came on board the "Black Hawk" to offer the information requisite. The route usually taken by traders, half-breeds, and individuals who attend the court at La Pointe, and by the carrier of the mail once a fortnight, is up the St. Croix River by a bark canoe some eighty miles to the small lake which forms its head-waters; thence there is a short portage to the Bois Brulé River, which empties into Lake Superior fifty miles above La Pointe; this is descended, and the voyagers coast the rest of the way. The trip takes seven, eight, or ten days—the coasting along Lake Superior being difficult work when it is rough. The voyageurs are paid for their time going and returning. The canoes are poled, and the current being strong, they cannot make more than twenty-five or thirty miles a day up stream. Another route sometimes taken is up the St. Croix to Kettle River, one of its branches, and up that as far as practicable; and thence by a long portage to St. Louis River and Fond du Lac. But neither of these routes afford sufficient in the way of scenery to compensate for the fatigue and expense, unless the mere love of wild adventure be strong enough to form an inducement.

The region between St. Croix River and Millelacs has been called a "Golgotha," on account of the bloody strife between the Dakotas and Ojibwas or Chippewas. After a great battle in 1841, the Indians of Pokeguma went to live with their countrymen near Lake Superior. Lake Pokeguma, four or five miles long, and two wide, is strewn with boulders, and tall, hoary pines grow to the water's edge. It is on Snake River, twenty miles above the Falls of St. Croix.

On our return, we made a call for an hour or so at the house of Mr. Ansell Smith, about three miles below the Falls. To this intelligent gentleman I am indebted for the local information I have recorded. Coming two years before, he had found a deep forest on his present location; now his nearly finished framed house overlooks a large vegetable garden on the river bank; money is brought into circulation by the constant employment and high wages of laborers, and he sees the barges, bearing stores, pass his house nearly every day. By another year a good road for travelling will probably be opened to Stillwater. At this time, the mail was carried on horseback once a week. In winter there is continual passing to and fro on the ice. It is a mistake, he said, to suppose the winters in Minnesota the dullest seasons; they are much the liveliest, every man being then more at leisure, and the closing, by freezing, of the lakes and rivers making the air so dry that an intense degree of cold may be borne without inconvenience. Labor in the open air was not suspended in the winter of 1851–2, even though at one time the degree of cold was so great that the mercury became solid; while in a moister region, or where the wind sweeps across the prairies, work cannot be performed when the thermometer stands 40° higher.

Mrs. Smith—a very charming woman, kindly presented me with some pretty agate pebbles from a stream near, and a sack made by the Chippewas, of braided strips of bark, in a shape rudely resembling a pappoose, filled with the wild rice which is one of the staples of the territory. This grain grows in great abundance about the head-waters of the St. Croix and its tributaries, on the northern branches of the Mississippi, and in all the lakes in the northern part of Minnesota. Where the water is shallow and of nearly uniform depth, it often forms an unbroken field of thousands of acres. When growing, it somewhat resembles Indian corn, though the stalk is more slender, attaining the average height of ten or twelve feet. "It forms with fish and maple sugar the principal subsistence of the Chippewas." They sell large quantities to the whites, some preferring it to the common rice of the south, and considering the unfitness of the soil on which it grows for any other crop, it may become a profitable article of commerce. The mode of collecting it is as follows:

"In the first place, to protect it from blackbirds, they collect the grain in bunches while it is in the milk, and cover each bunch with a band made of the bark of the linden or basswood tree. When the grain is sufficiently matured, the band is cut and removed, and one person, with a long pole, bends down the heads over the canoe in which he is seated, while another, with a pole, threshes off the grain. In this way some families gather fifty bushels. The time of gathering commences about the first of August and lasts six weeks. They dry it by placing it on mats on a scaffold over a fire. When sufficiently dry, a hole is dug in the ground, and about a bushel of rice is put in it and covered with a deer skin. A man steadying himself by a stake driven into the ground, jumps about on the grain until the hulls are removed. The women then winnow it out with a fan made of birch bark." *

A little below Mr. Smith's the steamboat grounded

* Seymour.

on the same sand-bar which had detained us twenty-four hours in ascending the river, and after some discussion the party from the Marine determined on proceeding in a small bateau. They invited me to join them, one of the ladies kindly proffering hospitality for the night, or as long a time as the steamer might stay on the bar—and promising to show me the curiosities of scenery in the neighborhood. A pleasant company was presently gathered in the little craft which, paddled by one of the gentlemen at either end, shot rapidly down the river. It was a mode of transit peculiarly Western, and had to me the charm of novelty and romance. We glided among the islands, following a less devious course than the larger boats, and stopped awhile at the rocky base of a bluff, to drink of a spring pouring out its crystal treasures, and examine the poles of a Chippewa wigwam, which appeared not to have been long deserted. Had time permitted, a walk the whole distance would have been delightful. But as we caught a distant view of the Marine, the "Black Hawk" could be seen just above us; on she came, her great engine puffing like a monster out of breath; in vain our paddles were plied to win the race; she strode over the waters, swept the sand-bar that impeded her progress, and only checked her course for an instant to avoid running down our daring little bark, that crossed directly under her bows. We followed in her wake, and notwithstanding the attractions of the social circle at the Marine, I was glad to have the prospect of reaching St. Paul early the next morning.

The occurrence of a steamboat landing at Willow River, seemed to stir the whole town; a hundred of the residents sprang on board the moment we touched the landing, and many ascended to the ladies' cabin and even peered into the state-rooms. This seemed a singular exhibition of curiosity, many of the boats from Galena making regular trips to Stillwater on their way to St. Paul.

Mr. Ansell Smith has favored me with a description of the valley and tributaries of the St. Croix, and as this interesting region is almost unknown, although destined to become an important part of our country, I give it at some length. Immediately west of the bluff overlooking Taylor's Falls, extends a forest consisting of the usual varieties of timber growing elsewhere in the same latitude; chiefly the sugar maple, linn, oak, elm, ash, birch, poplar, and butternut, with an almost impenetrable undergrowth, mostly of prickly ash and small blue beech. The common beech and hemlock, so prevalent in some of the Eastern States, are here never seen. The woods increase in density as you proceed westward, leaving the river. The ground, though undulating, is sufficiently level for agricultural purposes; the soil a rich, black, sandy loam. This forest tract is said to include an area of not less than two hundred square miles, running parallel with the river for about twenty miles, and extending ten or twelve miles back.

This body of timber forms the eastern border of the waters of the Sunrise, running in a north direction and emptying into the St. Croix some seventy miles from its junction with the Mississippi. This is the first western tributary of the St. Croix worthy of notice; the absence of western branches below its mouth being caused by the superior elevation of the land in the immediate vicinity of the St. Croix. The valley of the Sunrise is now attracting considerable attention, and is represented by those who have visited it as one of the most beautiful and fertile in the Northwest. Mr. William Holmes, who can claim the honor of being the earliest pioneer, is building on the bank of the Sunrise, about ten miles from its mouth. From that point the stream varies from fifty to seventy-five feet in width, and is inclosed between banks some twenty feet high, sloping gradually on either side to the water's edge. It is rapid enough to afford abundance of water-power for manufacturing purposes. On its west side extends for many miles a beautiful prairie, sprinkled with small groves. Ascending this river, we find it deeper and slower, its serpentine course being in the midst of a valley fifty or sixty rods wide, and covered with luxuriant wild grass, through which, at intervals, run clear rills from the springs gushing out along the ridges.

Near the mouth of the Sunrise there is a stopping place for teams passing to the pineries with supplies for the lumbermen, and a few settlers are opening farms in the neighborhood. Its local advantages will render this a central point for a considerable portion of the surrounding country. The road from Point Douglas to Lake Superior laid out by Government, which thus far runs near the St. Croix, is here separated from it by a bend in the river.

The next tributary—a stream called Goose Creek—has low banks, which are liable to be overflowed, and wanders through fine meadow lands promising as rich a reward for the labor of the husbandman, especially in stock-raising and dairy products, as any portion of Minnesota, or indeed of the United States. Hitherto the supplies carried into the woods, of beef, pork, corn, flour, butter, etc., have been purchased at Galena and other points below on the Mississippi—the expenses of transportation five or six hundred miles by water, and by land carriage to the place of destination, with the profit of the speculator, being added to the original cost of each article. The heavy tax to which the consumer is thus subjected may open a fair prospect to the home producer, especially in view of the fact that the home competition for years to come cannot effect any material reduction in prices.

Ten or twelve miles further up, passing over a barren tract covered with scanty vegetation, we come to Rush Creek, a small clear stream running through a body of hardwood timber. Half a day's travel further will bring us to Snake River. This and Kettle River, some miles northward, are the two largest and most important western tributaries of the St. Croix—each being, at its junction, nearly as large as the parent stream. Snake River drains a large extent of country, some of its branches extending far to the southwest, and interlocking with the northern branches of Rum River, southward of Millelacs or Spirit Lake, while others collect the stray rivulets as far north as the county of Itasca. This tract is chiefly covered with

pine, mingled with hardwood, like the other best pineries of this region. The amount of pine lumber annually cut on Snake River and its branches, probably exceeds fifteen million feet. The lumbermen now confine their operations within a short distance of the banks of the streams, to save the expense of extra hauling; but the pine growing further back is generally considered of better quality.

The United States road, as surveyed, crosses Snake River near Pokeguma Lake. Here was formerly a mission established for the conversion and education of the Indians, which has lately been abandoned. "The mission farm" was also cultivated at this place, and with "Greeley's Farm," which affords a stopping place for teamsters, is the only sign of improvement hereabouts; in fact, there is yet no permanent settlement north of Sunrise. Kettle River,—of which less is known—rises in Wisconsin, thence taking a southerly course with sufficient bearing westward to carry it through a portion of Minnesota, and joining the St. Croix a little below the point where the latter stream begins to form the boundary line between Wisconsin and Minnesota. A large part of Kettle River lying north of the Chippewa treaty line, the labors of lumbermen have extended but a few miles from its mouth.

Above the point where it becomes the boundary, the St. Croix being so reduced as to be fordable—Wisconsin steps across and takes a line due north for the falls on St. Louis River. The Badger State—says Mr. Smith—is a very good neighbor, but when we reflect that she has been so grasping as to cut us off entirely from the southern shore of Lake Superior, and compel us to go round the falls to reach the navigable waters of St. Louis River, we feel that she might have treated her infant sister with a little more indulgence. Commercially and socially, the northern part of Wisconsin, including that bordering on Lake Superior, and the whole St. Croix valley, is connected with Minnesota.

Ascending the St. Croix in a northeasterly direction, and passing several unimportant tributaries, we find it a small clear stream, the outlet of a beautiful sheet of water called St Croix Lake by way of distinction from the lower—Lake St. Croix. A short portage from this point, as before mentioned, carries us to the Bois Brulé, so called from the pine woods burnt on its banks. One unacquainted with the navigation of these brooks, would marvel at the patience and perseverance of the voyageurs. Sometimes walking in the stream, they drag their birchen vessels, or increase the depth of water by a temporary dam, and when there is no water, carry the light canoes and the lading on their backs, till they find a place where the craft can be launched. Schoolcraft says of the Brulé: "Any other person but one who had become familiar with northwest portages, would be apt to say, on being ushered to this secluded spot, 'Well, this is certainly an eligible place to quench one's thirst at, but as for embarking on this rill, with a canoe and baggage, the thing seems to be preposterous.' And so it certainly appeared on our arrival. There was not an average depth of water of more than two to four inches; but by going some distance below, and damming the stream, it rose, in a short time, high enough to float a canoe, with a part of its lading. The men, walking in the stream, then led the canoes, cutting away the brush to veer them, and carrying such parts of the lading as could not, from time to time, be embarked."

Turning southward, we come to the Nemakagon, the first eastern tributary of St. Croix worth attention. The yellow or Norway pine here grows in considerable quantities, and traces of lumbermen are visible. The white pine grows further south and west. The other eastern tributaries deserving mention are Yellow, Clam, Wood, Trade, and Apple Rivers—the last joining the St. Croix a few miles above Stillwater. Pine abounds on all these streams, which take their rise in the same extensive pinery, probably, that covers the head waters of Willow and Chippewa Rivers; though for some distance before entering the main river they flow through a sterile tract, supposed to have been once covered with pine forest, afterwards consumed by fire. A few isolated trees remain, degraded, from the lofty honors of their ancestry, and the desolate plains are covered for miles with blue or whortle berries, affording a rich feast to the weary traveller. Near the Falls and on the east side is a large body of hardwood timber, the soil being generally of the best quality for cultivation. Six miles below the Falls we strike a rich and fertile prairie, or more properly a succession of prairies, separated by groves, and extending far southward. This prairie is occupied by enterprising farmers, and the luxuriant crops are a sufficient guarantee for the fertility of the soil; the high prices obtained for produce indicating the wisdom of the settler in choosing this location. Wheat of the first quality has been raised, though there are no flouring mills nearer than Bowles', on Lake St. Croix, nearly forty miles distant.

The St. Croix Valley, like other portions of Minnesota, is remarkable for its numerous lakes. Chisago Lake, from which the county takes its name, one of the most beautiful in the territory—is about ten miles west of Taylor's Falls by the road; it is triangular in form, divided by a peninsula into two parts, each forming a lake, connected by a strait, and with its various indentations, presents not less than fifty miles of coast. "Norberg's Peninsula"—so called from the first claimant on it, who came in the spring of 1851, is nearly a mile in length, but narrow, including only about one hundred acres, and covered with a dense growth of sugar-maple and other timber. Its banks are twenty-five or thirty feet high, but not precipitous. Opposite Norberg's, and near the main peninsula dividing the two lakes, is Van Rensselaer's Island. A visit to this spot in the spring of 1851, when it formed the dividing line between savage and civilized life, was interesting. Several Swedish families had commenced opening their farms in the neighborhood, and the sound of the axe, the occasional falling of a tree, the smoke curling above the forest, the flight of wild fowl across the lake, and the shrill scream of the loon, proved the first invasion of the primeval solitude. Mr. Van Rensselaer soon after took possession of the island, which contained seven or eight acres, built a neat log house, and brought into it a well selected library. He has since cleared and cultivated part of the land, and with his favorite Shakspeare and other books, leads an independent and happy bachelor's life, though he is the only American living in the vicinity of the lake.

Another distinctive feature of the St. Croix region, common to the whole territory—is its marshes and swamps. These may be classed as hay-meadows, tamarac swamps, and cranberry marshes: each having its particular value. The early settler finds the natural hay-meadow very convenient; the tamarack swamps, affording material for fencing and timber for building, are equally important; and from the cranberry marsh the farmer not only gathers a supply of fruit for his own family use, but finds a crop of which he can always dispose at good prices. These berries will no doubt become a leading article of exportation from Minnesota. They are gathered with rakes so constructed as to let the vines pass between the teeth while retaining the fruit, and a single person may sometimes gather two or three barrels in a day. The average price is five dollars a barrel.

Another kind of marsh is usually covered with moss, and a hard wiry kind of grass, and woe to the traveller whose way lies across it, for the deceitful ooze covers water some feet deep, and the quivering foundation gives warning of a liquid region still below. Many of these marshes are susceptible of drainage.

The chief exported article from the region described must for a long time be pine lumber. Thirty-five teams have been engaged in logging during the winter of 1852–3 on the St. Croix and its tributaries.

Each team usually consists of four yoke of oxen, for which ten laborers make up the complement of hands. It was estimated that 105,000 logs, making thirty-five million feet of lumber, would be cut the last season; three thousand logs or a million feet, being a fair winter's work for one team. Of this amount about fifteen million feet are sawed at the different mills on St. Croix River and Lake, before being sent to market, twenty million being rafted and sent below in logs. The chief market is St. Louis, though many logs are sold at Rock Island and different points on the Mississippi.

The proceeds of the St. Croix lumber trade for the season of 1852–3 have been estimated as follows:

15,000.000 feet of sawed lumber	at $12 per m.	$180,000
20,000,000 feet of logs	at $ 9 per m.	$180,000
10,000,000 lath	at $2.50 per m.	$ 25,000
Making a gross income of		$385,000

Nor is there any business the proceeds of which are more generally distributed, for these find their way through different avenues to persons engaged in almost every variety of occupation. To the farmer is afforded a home market for his produce; and employment to the laborer at the season when his time is generally worth least; while the labors of the blacksmith, shoemaker and tailor, are also brought into requisition; the competition being not so much in cheapness as in quality.

X.

PASSING an hour or two beside the Falls on the side of the river opposite the town of St. Anthony, and at the hospitable residence of Col. Stevens, we had a walk and conversation with an intelligent lady who had spent three years in teaching in the vicinity, and had witnessed the growth of the largest towns in the Territory. The Indians, with whom the region was then populous, gave her a name signifying "the book-woman"—from the number of books she distributed among the ignorant and destitute. She related amusing anecdotes of one "brave" who aspired to the honor of her hand. He would spend hours in serenading her with his flute, according to the Indian fashion of making love, and would come to her school, in which there were several half-breeds, and prevail on these to interpret his wooing. His promises to "build her wigwam and hunt the deer, and make her moccasins," did not incline her heart towards him, yet she wished to treat him kindly, and in return for a pewter ring with which he presented her, gave him a bunch of shining brass ones. Her surprise was great when, a few days after, he came to fetch home his bride, the exchange of rings being the Indian form of betrothal. On her refusing to go with him, he departed, and the next day sent several stout warriors to bring her—expressing great disappointment and chagrin when it was explained to him that he had no right to consider himself her lord and master. His next appearance was in front of her school-house at the head of an armed troop of savages; but on her appealing to him with gestures of entreaty, not to terrify the children, he went away without molesting any one.

It was with much regret we bade farewell, for the present, to Minnesota. Pleasant will be our memories of that pleasant region. While waiting at the Rice House for the signal of departure, a note was brought in, proffering information concering the route from La Pointe to the Falls of St. Croix; a gentleman who had just accomplished a canoe voyage to Stillwater, having heard of us and our inquiries while descending the St. Croix. The incident showed the general interest taken in strangers on a tour of observation.

The waters had been so long falling that it was necessary to go down the river some three miles in a flat boat, into which animate and inanimate freight was tumbled promiscuously, shelterless in the blaze of sunshine, beneath the gaze of an unwonted crowd assembled on the heights above the landing. It was, perhaps, the first demonstration toward a riot since the settlement of the place. The bless.d Maine Liquor Law being in operation, the authorities were about to seize and destroy a quantity of the contraband article still kept in a store on the edge of the bluff. The people had rushed together to rescue the liquor, and manifested so stern a determination to prevent the sacrifice, that it was rumored the city authorities would prudently forbear to provoke an altercation in which they were sure to come off second best. All was quiet in the assemblage as we slowly dropped down the river in our primitive barge. The bottom-lands we passed were lined with Indians, whose blue and scarlet blankets and head-dresses looked picturesque enough, half hidden by the trees. In the space of an hour and a half we were on board "The Nominee," and ploughing our way rapidly downward. The Nominee is one of the line owned by B. Campbell & Co., and is the finest boat on the Upper Mississippi; it has withal, an extensive reputation associated with the popularity of the excellent Capt. Orrin Smith, who has long been its commander.

Dr. J —— and his charming wife received us with a cordial welcome, and would allow us to stay nowhere but at their vinewreathed cottage, in one of the retired streets of Galena. This place cortainly merits a celebrity for the warmheartedness and social qualities of its inhabitants. Among the visitors who called upon us, it will not be impertinent to mention the name of Mrs. Harris, formerly Miss Coates, a lady whose lectures to women on Physiology have been celebrated in past years, and who is now residing here. Her graceful person and manners, and her low, musical voice could not fail from the first moment to charm us, and would have gone far to disarm prejudice against female teachers of branches of learning long appropriated to

masculine investigation. The conversation turning upon "Woman's Rights Conventions," we ventured frankly to express our rooted aversion—conservatives as we were—even to the name of any such thing. But when asked if we could not see that many reforms were necessary to place women on an equal footing with men in facilities for earning a subsistence, if we could not think of many occupations suited to woman's ability and retiring modesty, from which she is now excluded and forced to more galling and ill-paid labors; if superior advantages of education should not be afforded to woman in all classes, and if no necessity existed for her protection from the cruel and crushing wrongs inflicted by domestic tyranny—then we were compelled to admit that she has *not* her "rights" as a human being. The lady had evidently the better of us, but she was meek in her triumph, and only counselled us hereafter to be more candid than to condemn "conventions" laboring to reform the evils of the existing state of society, notwithstanding that there might be much to censure in their proceedings and their ultra notions on the subject.

We were much gratified in attending service at the Second Presbyterian Church in this city on Sunday, and hearing an excellent sermon from Rev. Mr. W——, in which sound doctrine was explained in connection with the noble Christian precepts by which the heart and life are to be regulated. I have frequently had occasion to observe how much more of the great truths of the Christian system is unfolded in the sermons of Southern and Western divines than in the intellectual essays which are too often substituted, in our eastern cities, for the preaching of the living word. This is not the place, however, to speak on this subject as I could wish.

One not experienced can scarcely form an idea of the difference made in the aspect and movement of things in general in towns upon or near the Mississippi, by the state of the waters. The convenience and enjoyment of almost every individual is affected by it. We felt the depression from Minnesota to Illinois, on the right hand and on the left. Passing up Fêvre River with a wake of mud, we saw the stream shrunken into pitiable limits —its waste of bank on either side, wetted by the rush of water forced up by the passage of boats, a broad line of black mud. Still the parched earth drank no nourishment from the heated air, and the summer sun exacted his tribute from the streamlets, and the foliage began to look sere and withered, and people to talk ominously of the long drought, and the heavy rate of freights. There, at Galena, lay the West Newton, and other first class boats, laid up till the next rise, while smaller boats labored in and out, each bringing intelligence of still greater difficulty of progress.

We improved inevitable delay by a visit to an agreeable family residing five miles distant among the diggings. The shaft we descended was about seventy feet deep, and one by one we were let down in a tub by the windlass. At the bottom were horizontal drifts, the roof and sides of which were studded with the shining metal. Each mine has two openings for ventilation, and work is best done in the winter, when miners do not suffer from the "damps." A few years since a human bone was found thirty feet below the surface, its interior filled with beautiful spar.

After several contingent adieus, the boat which expectant passengers had crowded in haste on Monday morning, at five the next afternoon left the wharf, toiling along at a rate not so rapid as a brisk walk. There was a sensible moderation in the heat; our little party was a very agreeable one, and in time the full moon saw us on our way down the Mississippi. The numerous sand-bars make the channel tortuous; but the boat was of light draught, and daylight found us a little below Hampton, at the head of the Upper Rapids. Here our good fortune forsook us; we were fast on rocks from which no labor or effort could set free the struggling vessel. The hours of the day wore by in one unsuccessful attempt after another, and another morning discovered us in precisely the same position. The passengers in the ladies' cabin read what few books they had brought with them, gossiped idly on matters and things in general, or napped away the time; those who had babies nursed them, and the diversion of three meals a day—an excellent table being set, according to custom on the western boats—was hailed as an appropriate and welcome pastime. The breeze came pleasantly, meanwhile, as a friendly visitor to tell of sweet nooks on the land, of wooded islets, and flower-covered prairies in the distance, and lakes perchance, and dancing rivulets fresh from the cool embrace of sunless woods. A steamboat appeared in the distance—laboring along the narrow, winding channel upward, and hopes were entertained that the swell of the waters as she passed would lift us from our involuntary perch. On she came, laden with passengers assembled on the decks to gaze at our forlorn plight; proudly she swept by, almost brushing the side of our craft, and when just ahead, turned, while her course was suddenly checked. She was certainly intending to tow us back! But, no! after a few moments her bow was again turned up stream; and she left behind her a wake of foam—the subsiding swell leaving us tugging at our anchor as hopelessly as before.

Three more steamboats passed up in the time we lay on the rocks; one, our well beloved Nominee, sent down the river for repairs previous to resuming her regular trips to St. Paul. In the afternoon of the second day, more strenuous efforts were made for our liberation; the freight had been removed to a barge—the passengers were directed to come forward, and, with mighty struggles, the huge vessel was at last shoved off by degrees, till we were once more plowing the waters, with cheered hearts, looking forward to the prospect that should open on our arrival at Montrose. During the lowness of the river, the steamers from Galena are obliged to terminate their trips at that point, passengers proceeding thence by stage twelve miles, to Keokuk, where they meet the larger packets. It was eight in the evening before we arrived at Montrose, and for seventy or eighty passengers there was only one stage, a barouche or two, and a small bateau. While apprehension prevailed as to our further progress, it was announced that a flat-boat would soon be in readiness; it was large and cumbrous, but could not be made to draw more than six inches of water, loaded as it was with trunks and boxes, and forty or fifty passengers. An awning extended in gondola fashion over part of the boat, and in the stern a weather-tight room was boarded up, which contained a cooking stove and one or two mattresses, on which sundry babies reposed after the fatigues of the day. It was a wild moonlight excursion, this floating down with the current, now and then striking the rocks of the rapids, or passing a shoot rapidly, or twisting and striving among the breakers. As we neared Keokuk, several runners on the banks set forth the merits of the rival boats—the St. Paul and the Kate Kearney—in voluble recommendations. "Not a bug to be seen—will give the passage if you find one"—was music in our ears, after the doleful experiences of the last three nights, when, driven from the staterooms by the "native population" we had been constrained to take on the cabin floor such rest as could be obtained amid the voluble chattering of Irishwomen, who seemed to think they could not have their money's worth unless they murdered the sleep of every body else. Another grievance felt only by a fastidious few, grew out of the fact that few of the staterooms were supplied with ewers and basins, the occupants of the others being expected to perform their ablutions in a small wash-room, scantily supplied with water and towels, and allowed but a minute and a half for the duty, elbowed and grumbled at in the mean

time by half a dozen impatient for the succession. This was uncomfortable enough for those who could be content with "a wipe" over the prominent parts of the face, and an imperfect cleansing of the hands; but for us whom the habitual and plenteous use of the Croton had made absolutely dependent for life and comfort on a daily *bonâ fide* bath—the evil was intolerable. We had no resource but to brave the cabin-maid's frowns and a general stare, by seeking an introduction to the concealed water barrel, filling stolen or borrowed pitchers to the brim, carrying them resolutely to our staterooms, and fastening the door. I must record my conviction that the duty of cleanliness is sadly neglected by the generality of tourists. The poorest boats would be better provided with conveniences for washing, were these required or used; but most passengers are satisfied with the limited facilities afforded. Our ablutions being regarded as an extraordinary innovation on established custom, we did not wonder at hearing one woman say she "felt very mean," and another, that "travelling never seemed to do any good" to her or her family.

At length we were swung alongside the St. Paul, a new and beautiful boat, sumptuously furnished. The scenery of the Mississippi is merely pleasing, but not of striking beauty, between Galena and the Illinois River. The site of Davenport and Rock Island, at the foot of the upper rapids, is imposing, and the range of hills surrounding those towns form a fine background to the picture. The island, with the deserted buildings of Fort Armstrong—the locality of the murder of Col.

Davenport—is always pointed out, and arrests the eye as the most remarkable object in the vicinity. At the mouth of the Illinois the bluffs rise to the height of one hundred and fifty or two hundred feet, and become precipitous, with the same castellated appearance observed above Dubuque. These columnar fronts are often so regular as to resemble architectural ruins. This formation continues nearly all the way to Alton.

It was eleven o'clock, a bright moonlight night, when we landed at Alton. The stillness was remarkable for so large a town, and but one person could be seen on the large wharf; it was the porter of the Franklin House, who placed the luggage on his barrow and silently led the way to the hotel. In the morning we were welcomed to the hospitable home of a kind relative—Rev. Mr. L.—who resided in what is called the Middle town. This city of Alton is divided into three distinct villages—the Lower town, the place of business, being more compactly built on rugged eminences and declivities, somewhat after the fashion of Galena; the Middle, a long mile distant, composed of more aristocratic country residences, each furnished with spacious grounds and gardens; and the Upper built in a similar manner. A large business is done in the place, and it is pervaded by an air of vitality. A packet plies twice a day between it and St. Louis.

After a visit of a day or two in Alton, my cousin accompanied me in a drive to Bunker Hill, about seventeen miles distant. He had been one of the earliest residents of the State, and his pioneer recollections were interesting. Not far from Alton we passed by the site of Fort Edwards. This was standing in 1813, when it afforded protection to the hardy border settlers from the prowling Indian. It stood in Madison County, Illinois, three miles from the Mississippi River, in the midst of a deep forest, its blockhouses and other buildings made of stout hewn logs, its pickets a rampart of thick saplings, strong enough to defy the assault of musketry, and the smooth green of its inclosure, in the midst of which was a well of the rude fashion of the olden time, shadowed by the farspreading boughs of lofty trees without. The only memorial of this primitive military post is a drawing taken by an accomplished lady residing at Paddock's Grove, about ten miles distant; she also furnished me with the story which has made that spot memorable in Western tradition.

Before the outbreak of the last war with Great Britain, Abel and George Moore, two brothers from the Carolinas, paddled their way up the Mississippi with their families and goods, and landed not far from the site of Lower Alton. They made their way with difficulty through the tangled woods three miles into the interior in the forks of Wood River, a pretty stream flowing through the prairies lying several miles towards the east. Here in time, log cabins, chinked with clay, with mud and stick chimneys, were built; fields were cleared and planted, and vegetables filled the little gardens. The dwellings were about half a mile distant each from the other, with woods between; but a well-trodden trail led from house to house. The Moores and their neighbors frequently heard of Indian depredations committed in other settlements, but living in so remote and secluded a locality, they felt little apprehension. This delusive confidence marked the spot forever as the scene of a murder; the atrocity of which is not exceeded in the annals of savage warfare.

On a bright Sabbath day the two children of one of the Moores came with an aunt to their uncle's cabin to play with their young cousins. Towards evening the children asked permission to visit a neighbor whose farm lay just back of the Moores', and four of them went away in high spirits, accompanied by their aunt, who promised to bring them home before dusk. When the evening was far advanced, and they did not return, the consciousness of imprudence in suffering them to venture alone, for the first time struck Moore and his wife, and he set off for his brother's cabin, thinking the little party might have gone thither from the neighbor's. This hope was disappointed; they had not been there since the morning. The other Moore called two men, and the four, carrying their guns, went into the woods to search for the missing ones. Mrs. Moore, as soon as her husband, brother-in-law, and the two men had left her cabin, unable to bear the tortures of suspense, resolved to go out herself, and bridling a horse from the stable she mounted without a saddle, and riding at full speed dashed into the woods. She made her way notwithstanding the darkness, along the well marked trail, but had not rode far before the gleam of something white in the path arrested her attention. Flinging herself from the horse and laying her hand on the object, she felt something soft, warm and quivering. A moment turned her breathless suspense into horrible certainty;—it was the body of her beloved sister! At a flash she comprehended the full extent of the awful calamity. The imminent danger in which she herself stood, she heeded not. Again mounting her horse, she rode on till she met the four men, to whom she communicated her terrible discovery, and when they had procured lights, went back with them to the place of death.

It was as she had anticipated; the yet warm, but lifeless corpses of the sister and the four children lay scalped and shockingly mangled. It was a fearful scene—that ghastly disclosure—the glare of the torches on the ensanguined forms of the murdered innocents—the black darkness around—the forest boughs shutting out the sky—the grief and horror in the faces of the living! The dear remains were reverently lifted from the bloody ground, two more men—the six constituting the whole neighborhood—having been sent for, and were conveyed to the house where they had spent the day so pleasantly. Shortly after midnight the men had prepared a single grave to receive the five slaughtered ones; and then they armed themselves and went forth in pursuit of the Indians, leaving the two bereaved mothers to perform the last sad offices for the dead. "More than thirty years"—Mrs. Moore has been heard to say—"have passed away since that terrible night, and the mournful day that followed it, yet the memory of the heart-rending scene is as vivid as if it had occurred but yesterday. Sister Moore and I went to work; collected all the pieces of split board we could find, and placed them in the bottom of the grave; then we brought fresh grass and leaves, and made a bed upon them with as much care as if we had been providing for the comfort of the dear children. After washing the clotted blood from what hair the removal of the scalps had left, and from their poor mangled bodies, we dressed them, and then laying their aunt first in the grave, placed two little ones on each side of her. We spread a sheet and quilt over them, and a covering of leaves and grass, and replaced the earth above them." It was but a few days after this mournful tragedy, that Gov. Edwards, then Governor of the Territory of Illinois, came with his rangers to the little settlement. The locality was selected for a fort, which was built shortly afterwards, and called Fort Edwards.

Bunker Hill is one of the most beautiful little villages in the State, situated on a prairie in high cultivation; the houses are neat and arranged tastefully, and each is garnished with a pretty garden and plenty of shade trees, which give the loveliest rural aspect imaginable to the whole place. I found here a welcome reception from a near relative, and a charming circle of kinsfolk, who had been expecting a visit of some weeks.

XI.

The advantages of a prairie location are very important to a farmer, but the aspect of a vast treeless plain, unrelieved by shade or flowing water, is any thing but inviting. This little village, situated in the heart of an extensive prairie—a part of the vast range stretching northward to Chicago—occupies the summit of the "roll;" the streets are shaded with stately trees, and the houses generally surrounded by shade trees and shrubbery. "Clay Cottage," the residence of my venerable aunt, is a rural paradise. The dwelling house, of substantial brick, painted light gray, peeps invitingly through a plantation of tall trees of several varieties—its verandah and trellised porch wreathed with roses and flowering vines, and a bordering of rare shrubs and rose trees completely embowering it. The smooth lawn is sprinkled with shrubbery, and a clustering grape-vine covers with its luxuriant drapery the whole of the rear buildings. On one side, the lawn terminates in a large flower garden filled with choice and beautiful plants; on the other, a grove of tall trees, carpeted with verdure, terminates in a park of locust trees so thickly planted that the sun cannot penetrate their recesses. This by confession the most elegant "place" in town, may represent the better order of prairie homes. A well is on the premises, and wood is easily brought from the "timber" a few miles distant. The fruit trees yield abundance of fruit; the wild prairie affords pasturage for the cows, and the breezes that sweep across the green, heaving expanse, are laden with health and invigorating power. Wild fruits are brought in every day for sale, and at the proper seasons, deer, wild turkeys and ducks, prairie fowl, partridges, &c., are offered. A specimen of the peaches was sent me, which measured eleven inches in circumference.

The population of Bunker Hill is about three hundred. The Alton and Terre Haute Railroad passes through the village, and the railroad from Al ton to Springfield, within seven miles. There is a Presbyterian and a Methodist church, and a Baptist congregation. The original name for the site was Wolf Ridge, on account of its elevated situation, and its being known as the haunt of a number of prairie wolves. It is not long since one of these animals was seen in the village. The inhabitants well remember the night prowlers at the doors of their cabins, in fear of which they were obliged every night to secure their provisions, if they would not have the bread snatched from their cupboards, or the meat from their larders. It ought to be added, that there is no lawyer in the village, and at present there seems no need of one. The only one who ever lived here was drowned in Wood River which he was crossing on horseback. A monument is being built to his memory.

There are two excellent practising physicians—Dr. H—— and Dr. E.

On the road leading to Woodburn, three miles westward, in a strip of timber bordering Wood Creek, stands an oak of towering height, which is called "the tree," by way of distinction. Woodburn is a village nearly as large as Bunker Hill, but not so pretty in appearance, and at this season in a dusty dishabille. No portion of the country feels the drought more than the prairie. The winds which sweep over it, unmoistened by streams and lakes, whirl clouds of dust from the trodden highway, and shake gustily the tops of the trees around the dwellings. In different directions extend beautiful drives, affording views of the wild and solitary prairie, boundless to the sight, yet sprinkled afar off with fields of tall corn and low white houses, each, doubtless, having its own story of change, and hardship, and labor, and hope to tell in the history of its inmates.

While driving out with one of my cousins, here and there we crossed the dry bed of a stream which at high water dashes merrily along, now parched up, so that the cattle, wandering over their immense pasture-ground, can find no water. A few forlorn geese had gone down into a cleft, and stood like topers pledging each other in a farewell, round a small puddle, the last remains of the shrunken stream, whose dry channel showed its former dimensions. At intervals a small frame dwelling, painted white and unrelieved by shade, peered up from the edge of the undulating landscape, requiring little stretch of fancy to be thought a sail on the bosom of an ocean-like expanse. But the settlers generally have had the good taste to plant trees for shade around their homes; and a cluster of them almost invariably denotes a civilized habitation.

About a mile and a half from the village is the home of a pioneer family, who removed from the neighborhood of Philadelphia some nineteen years ago, compelled by adverse circumstances to seek a home in western wilds. They had mingled in the refined circles of the city, and were accustomed to the luxuries of metropolitan life. The loss of property involved as they conceived, the loss of consideration, and in a kind of disgust with the world they resolved to bury themselves from the sight of their fellow creatures. The situation of their future home was chosen on the lone, wild prairie, far from human companionship or observation. A log cabin, well plastered with clay, was hauled from a distance; a chimney was built, and the first thing done was to dig a well and set out trees which might serve as a shelter from the burning sun. In the spring following a garden was laid out, the ground having been previously broken, and the plants which had been brought from the East, and kept in wet moss and earth, were set out.

Although bountiful nature has rewarded their labor, they still live in the primitive cabin which first received them, and retain their unsocial habits. Mrs. M—— will sometimes visit her neighbors, but welcomes none to her own dwelling; nor can any entreaty ever prevail on her to dine or take tea with an acquaintance; she cannot, she says, return the civility in a proper manner, and pride forbids her acceptance of it.

It was a warm afternoon when we drove thither, and fastening our horse at the gate, entered the inclosure. This was planted with trees, a dense cluster of which surrounded the cabin, which looked picturesque enough; in front the roof extended into a shed several feet wide, serving for a rustic portico; it was supported and shaded by the trees, and its extremity sheltered a well, by which the dripping bucket just drawn up by the windlass, stood offering the most refreshing beverage in the world. The sides of the cabin were hung with dried fruits of various kinds, different utensils for use, and articles of dress. In the single room were two beds, a table, and sundry chests, chairs, benches, etc.; there were two large glazed windows, and the remainder of the space was occupied with shelves, on which were heaped an unimaginable variety of articles. The chimney was built outside, and the wide hearth covered with substantial brick. There was a singular inconsistency between the rude aspect of this primitive home and the romantic beauty that surrounded it. The unmistakable impress of a delicate and refined taste was perceptible every where; in the artistic disposition of the trees and shrubbery, the careful veiling of all unsightly points, the rich smooth green of the grass, and the neat arrangement of the various outbuildings, all of which were sheltered by the softening foliage of the maple, redbud or locust. We were still more astonished when invited to walk into the flower-garden, to find it filled with the rarest and most exquisite specimens, such as would have done credit to the collection of a city florist. The younger lady made a selection of lovely flowers, and presented us each with a fragrant bouquet. An hour's conversation left us impressed with wonder at the cultivation evinced by persons who were content to live in so poor a dwelling. "Content" is hardly the word; for they have never ceased to regret the comforts of city life, nor become reconciled to their remote seclusion. Yet they prefer a home in the wilderness to living with reduced fortunes among their former friends, and desire no association with the neighbors who have clustered around them within a few years. "We are like Daniel Boone," said the old lady; "we have no longer room, the country is becoming too thickly settled." Yet probably none will come in sight during the term of her life.

A prairie home of a different character, stands on a considerable elevation two miles and a half from the village. The situation commands a very extensive view of the undulating landscape for many miles around, with the scattered white houses peering up at intervals on the edge of the horizon, and clumps of trees here and there denoting a residence of better pretensions. A thick grove of tall trees almost conceals from view a small framed house, behind which is a great field of standing corn, nearly twenty feet in height. A well almost dried up by the summer drought, is near the gate, and the shaded path winds upward to the door of the cabin, for it is no more, having but one room inside, with a loft. This room is occupied by two large beds, one of which is curtained off by a drapery of white sheeting, and a trundle bed is rolled out for the accommodation of a sick child. Two small tables, a chest, and a few split-bottom chairs, with a countless variety of smaller articles in housekeeping use, completed the furniture; the wide chimney-piece was stoutly defended with brick, and the plastered walls, discolored by time and hideously dirty, were somewhat less picturesque than the primitive sides of a log cabin. An unusual natural curiosity had made the place one of some resort. Two years since, three healthy infants, the offspring of one birth, lay in helpless innocence on one of the beds, appealing to the sympathetic care of curious visitors for a larger supply of clothing than had been provided in expectation of one.

Two of my relatives were pioneers some nineteen years ago, in this part of Illinois. Much of the furniture of their cabin was sent from Philadelphia, and included articles rarely seen in the backwoods, such as a carpet, sofa, etc. A neighbor who came in after it was arranged, expressed his surprise at the unusual quantity of "plunder," and in making his way to the ample fire-place, mounted on the chairs, and walked carefully from one to another around the room, treading as lightly as possible on the sofa. When asked why he did so, he answered,—"Because I don't want to dirty that 'ere nice coverlid." The attention of another was drawn to the carved feet of the sofa, and at length, moving gently towards it and stooping down to feel them, he exclaimed, "Bless me—if them aint bar's claws!"

Some incidents in the history of a family which I heard related hereabouts, are curiously romantic. A farmer, whom we shall call May, whose means were ampler than most new settlers', lived in 1812 in Illinois, about six miles from St. Louis. One morning early, a person then lodging in the house, who furnished this information, heard Mrs. May's voice in startled tones, calling to her husband to ask "What noise is that?" The drowsy husband answered, that the cry was probably that of an opossum or a screech owl. "Ah, no, John!" exclaimed the wife—"it is a young child!" She sprang from the bed, as did her husband, and both ran to the door; a basket was set on the doorstep, covered with a blanket, which Mrs. May removed, and there lay, imbedded in snow-white muslin and linen, a beautiful infant! Lifting it in her arms, she ran into the house, and laying it on her lap, examined its features with delighted curiosity, 'Is it not a beauty?" she cried, looking up in her husband's face: "and the way it has come is so funny!" The stern farmer replied, that he could see no fun in having other people's brats thrust upon him; but his grumbling was hushed by the benevolent woman, whose whole soul went forth in kindness towards the little helpless creature—evidently not more than four weeks old—thus cast on her maternal care. Notwithstanding the displeasure of Mr. May, which she knew to be more in appearance than reality, she kept her resolution of adding the trouble of providing for it to the charge of her own four children.

Matters went on thus for two or three years, and

the foundling, increased in beauty, became the pet of the household. Mr. May, however, treated the little girl with an indifference amounting to dislike, and manifested annoyance particularly when his wife would tell her visitors the child's brief history—always prefacing it by the exclamation—"the way the dear little thing came to us was so funny!" One day while he was alone in the room, he was playing with little Mary, when hearing his wife's step, he set her down quickly, pushing her from him. The child cried: Mrs. May took her up, and spoke complainingly of her husband's unkind treatment of the little desolate creature, whom he seemed to hate. "You are mistaken, Nancy," replied the farmer; "I do not hate the child; see, she knows I love her as much as yourself," and as he smiled and held out his arms, Mary sprang from the lap of her protectress and came to him, laughing merrily.

"But why, John, do you always treat the poor thing so unkindly?" asked the wife.

"I will tell you why, Nancy; because you tell everybody all about her; and it frets me to have people suppose I am bringing up nobody knows who, as my own; besides, it is a disgrace to the child! Now if you will agree to what I propose, I am willing, for the child's good, to sell out and move to one of the northern territories. But you must promise never to let any one know that we are not her parents, and never again to allude to the 'funny way' in which she came to us."

Mrs. May readily agreed to this generous proposal; the farmer sold out, and removed to what was then the territory of Michigan. We will now take up another portion of the story.

In one of the Eastern cities, a Mr. L—— and Miss C——, both of highly respectable families, had formed a matrimonial engagement with their parents' consent. But a wealthier suitor came, to whom the father, a stern and violent man, determined to wed his daughter. The lovers were secretly married, and arrangements were made with a respectable family going to Missouri, to take the bride with them, the husband who called himself her brother, promising to join them shortly. He left the city some time before Miss C——'s disappearance, and all believed that he had gone on a sea voyage. Soon after leaving home, Miss C—— wrote to inform her parents she was safe with friends, and had fled to avoid a compulsory marriage.

After a journey of several weeks, the young couple arrived at St. Louis. Notwithstanding the pains taken to conceal their movements, in a few months the father learned that his daughter was in the western country, and wrote to her that her mother, almost heart-broken at her loss, had fallen into ill health. Sincerely regretting his own unfeeling conduct, he entreated her to return in the spring, at which time he would send for her, having no suspicion that she was married. This letter was received by Mrs. L—— a short time previous to the birth of an infant, who was no other than the foundling aforementioned. She resolved to set off on her homeward journey as soon as her strength permitted. A journey in the spring, at that period, from St. Louis to Pittsburgh, was both difficult and dangerous; Mr. L—— expected to return, and he thought it best to leave their child, urging that the parents of his wife would be more readily conciliated by her returning apparently as she had left them; explaining all when she could choose a favorable time for so doing. The young mother could not bear the thought of parting with her little one; but feeling that she could never forgive herself should her mother die before she could return to receive her forgiveness and blessing, it appeared her duty to sacrifice her own feelings, and she at last consented.

Then occurred the question—with whom could the precious babe be trusted? The inhabitants of the place were mostly French, and they knew no trustworthy person who could be prevailed on to take charge of it. A young man, Mr. L.'s only intimate friend, was acquainted with Mr. and Mrs. May, and suggested that they would be certain to treat the child with all the tenderness its own parents could lavish on it, if their humanity were appealed to in its behalf as a deserted foundling. He engaged to deposit the infant, with all due circumstances of mystery, at their door, and report the manner of its reception; also to look after it faithfully in the absence of its parents.

The mother consented to the romantic scheme, and, packing the basket with as many clothes as it would hold—placing in the bottom a purse full of money—she set out with her husband and his friend, in the night, for May's house. Within a short distance of this they stopped, and with foreboding anguish, both kissed the baby's smooth cheek, and resigned it to their friend, endeavoring to console themselves with the belief that a year, at the furthest, would restore their darling to their arms. In a few days their friend called on Mr. May, saw how well the child was doing, heard the foster-mother say she loved and would cherish it as her own, and made a satisfactory report to its anxious parents.

Mr. and Mrs. L. immediately set off for the East, separating a few days before their arrival at the house of the wife's father. She was joyfully welcomed, and Mr. L. soon after received a letter inviting him to join her.

It was now about the commencement of the war with Great Britain, and as it was known the Indians would be troublesome on the frontier, it was arranged that Mr. L. should go immediately to the West, and bring the child to its mother. He reached St. Louis at a time when a general panic on account of the Indians had scattered the inhabitants. His friend had joined the rangers, and could nowhere be found; Mr. May's family had also disappeared; the neighbors had taken refuge in forts; and the most diligent inquiries failed in procuring the desired information. After some narrow escapes from the Indians, he was obliged to abandon the search, and return, disappointed and dispirited, to his unhappy wife. At the end of the war, both set out for the West, and landed at Shawneetown. From this point they travelled northward through Illinois, making diligent inquiries in every direction; for the hope of finding the lost one was not yet extinct in the mother's breast.

After travelling through the country for nearly a year, they discovered May's residence, and had the happiness of embracing the child whom separation had the more endeared to them. She was even more beautiful than the promise of her infancy, and very happy with her kind foster-parents, who had been preserved and prospered through all the troubles and dangers by which they had been surrounded. Mr. May was one of the most thriving farmers of Michigan. This little romantic episode in his history may not be known to his neighbors—for he was never very communicative—but it was the ground of a lasting friendship between his family and that of the little adopted one; both acknowledging from it a profitable lesson in life.

XII.

SOME ten miles from Bunker Hill, southward, is a country seat with rather elaborate surroundings of extensive gardens and park-like grounds, filled with trees of stately growth—regarded as the most aristocratic residence in the country for many miles around. The same family have occupied the premises between twenty and thirty years. Emigrating from New England, they located land in Illinois when it was but a territory, and its prairies were traversed by the wild savage. Their first abode was, as usual, a log cabin, patched with clay, with a mud and stick chimney built on the outside, and puncheon floor—the rough boards of the roof projecting a few feet in front, so as to form a shelter at the door from the falling rain or the noonday sun. This edifice is still preserved, and stands close behind the prouder mansion which is now the home of the pioneer family; a feeling of honorable pride inspiring them with a reverence for the humble dwelling which received the parents on their removal from the East.

All the neighbors within scores of miles remember the venerable Mrs. P——, as a true pioneer mother;

her industry, neatness, and thrifty management, and the orderly, unostentatious, dignified manner in which she discharged her matronly duties—sitting in some state at the head of her table, dressed in the old and simple fashion, and teaching her daughters to excel in those branches of housewifery which she had made to contribute so essentially to the comfort of all around her. Death removed her and the partner of her cares, and for years the house has been in possession of five unmarried daughters—the family having lately received an accession in a married sister, with her husband and children. The evidence of graceful female taste and care is seen in every part of the grounds and of the spacious mansion, which has long been noted as the seat of hospitality and charity. The flowers, shrubbery, and lawns are kept in the neatest order, and the plenteous table is seldom surrounded only by the family; visitors come from every quarter, and are always sure of receiving a genuine Western welcome. Our little party drove thither on a very warm day, passing through several strips of woodland bordering small streams, now dried up. At one point, the cry was suddenly raised, "A deer!" and a glance showed a splendid doe careering swiftly across the prairie, tossing her head as if to snuff the morning breeze, and clearing the way with such graceful bounds, that it must have been a hard heart that could have wished to cut short the enjoyment of so beautiful a creature by the deadly ball.

A large framed house by the roadside, half concealed in a plantation of locusts, was the abode of sickness; and while Dr. Ellet alighted and went in to see his patient, two of the Misses P—— came down the walk to greet us. They were on an errand of kindness, ministering to the sick neighbor, and expressed their regret at not being able to accompany us home. But the day was rendered agreeable by the hospitable attention of the other sisters. A white-haired old gentleman and his wife, their visitors, who were of Scottish birth, had known intimately Burns' "Highland Mary," and had some of her letters: and related anecdotes of the poet and his family. The heat of the day forbade extensive walks, but we lingered around the garden and shrubbery, and under the lofty trees, the shadows of which lay invitingly on the smooth grass, and listened to the history of a glorious pioneer woman of the West, which I shall record as a most interesting portion of the border annals of our country.

Mary Nealy was born on the 20th August, 1761, not far from Charleston, South Carolina. When she was very young, her father removed his family to Tennessee; the emigrants passing through Georgia to the place where now stands Chattanooga. The family was sent down the Tennessee River in canoes, taking with them their household stuff, clothes and provisions, while the father drove his horses and cattle along the banks; the two parties joining each other at the Muscle Shoals, whence they proceeded by land to the locality afterwards called Nealy's Bend, on the Cumberland River, near the site of Nashville. Our adventurous pioneer lived here several years. Mrs. Nealy took upon herself the task of teaching her daughters, hearing their spelling and reading lessons while she was busily spinning on her little wheel. When a school was established, the sons were sent three miles to attend it every day, the path through the woods being so infested with wolves that they were usually obliged to go on horseback.

After the commencement of the Revolutionary struggle, the family, with others in the neighborhood, sought refuge in a fort; the men venturing out as opportunity permitted, to attend to the cattle and cultivate their fields. Nealy was engaged in making salt, and was sometimes assisted by his daughter Mary, or Polly, as she was called. On a Sabbath morning in the fall of 1780, the young girl, wearing her Sunday dress, left the station in company with her father, and walked with him to the bank of the river. Mary happened to be standing at some little distance from her father, when she suddenly heard the report of a gun, and saw him fall to the ground. She had only time to see an Indian leap from his covert, when she lost her consciousness in a swoon. On her recovery, she found herself in the grasp of two of the savages, who were dragging her off with all possible haste, evidently apprehensive of pursuit from the station, which was at no great distance. No aid came, however, and the helpless girl was compelled to go on with her captors. They were three days without food; at length a bear was killed, and a piece of flesh given to the starving captive, which she ate raw. This imprudence pro-

duced severe illness, which was relieved by drinking a quantity of the bear's oil, according to Indian prescription.

The prisoner was offered her choice between becoming the wife of the chief's son, or the slave of his oldest wife; she chose the latter, and soon made herself so useful that the savages determined to spare her life. The party continued some time in Tennessee and Kentucky, and often encamped in canebrakes. One night, in attempting to escape—for the hope of finding her way back to home and friends was still cherished by the unfortunate girl—after leaving the encampment, she chanced to step on a sharp fragment of cane, which ran entirely through her foot. She was of course recaptured, and suffered the extremest agony from the wound, which was not entirely healed for months afterwards. During this time, having learned something of the Indian language, she frequently heard the advice given to kill and scalp her, rather than be troubled with a poor cripple; and it is probable nothing saved her but her knowledge of sewing and other kinds of work, which made her a valuable servant to her mistress.

One night when the Indians had encamped on the bank of a small stream, a heavy storm came on. To obtain shelter, Mary climbed into a tree completely canopied by a luxuriant grape-vine. In a short time after she had thus secured herself, a fierce gust of wind uprooted a large tree near by, and it fell with a tremendous crash, immediately over the place she had quitted. She heard the savages calling to her amidst the darkness and the driving storm, and when they received no answer, ascertained by their exclamations that they supposed she had been killed. A flash of joy penetrated her heart; here was an opportunity of escape! She remained still, while the Indians called and shouted repeatedly; but when they were silent, fear began to shake her new-born hopes. She had been severely punished for the previous attempt, and threatened with the tomahawk if it were ever repeated. Should she leave the tree, the dogs would in all probability discover her, and give the alarm. Uncertain what to do, she remained in the tree all night, not answering the calls which were repeated at intervals, in hopes the Indians would break up camp and depart before day, as they always did when apprehensive of pursuit. She was found, however, and compelled to accompany them in their northward course, and having crossed the Ohio, gave up in despair the faint hope that had remained in her breast, of being restored to her kindred. Fortune seemed to delight in mocking her with opportunities by which she could not profit. One night when they had encamped, a snow-storm came on, and she was completely covered by a snowdrift. In the morning, as the Indians were preparing to continue their journey, she could be found nowhere, and they concluded she had gone off during the night. Their anger was loudly expressed, and the most terrible tortures threatened, if she should again fall into their power. Hearing all this imperfectly, and only understanding that she was wanted, Mary rose from under her white coverlet in the very midst of the infuriated savages, whose shouts of astonishment and merriment, when they discovered the truth, were absolutely deafening. It was a bitter thought to her, that had she known how securely she was concealed, she might have remained in safety. The morning meal of the Indians was a large black snake, which was roasted and divided. A few inches only fell to the poor girl's share, but the piquant sauce of hunger made it seem delicious food. She was always permitted to share in every thing with her captors.

At one time, when the men were all absent from the camp, a large deer was seen making directly towards it. The old chief's wife ordered Mary to take a gun and shoot the animal, as she was known to be the best shot among all the women. The chief had expressly forbidden firing, on pain of death, in the absence of his men, the discharge of a gun being the appointed signal of the near approach of an enemy, and Mary hesitated to obey; but being urged, she fired, and shot the deer. In a few moments the Indians came rushing in, expecting to encounter the foe; and, when informed that it was a false alarm, the chief raised his tomahawk to kill the white girl who had dared to disobey his commands. His wife threw herself between him and the intended victim, exclaiming that she herself was the offender; but for a moment, as the uplifted weapon was whirling several times round the Indian's head, Mary expected he would bury it in her own. Perhaps the prospect of plenty of savory venison for supper did something to pacify the angry warrior.

At another time, when, by some means or other, the smallpox was introduced among the party, the captive became desperately ill with the terrible disease. For ten days she was entirely blind, being left alone in a lodge built for her at some distance from the camp, near a spring. Her food was brought and left at the spring, to which she would grope her way once in twenty-four hours. Her sufferings were somewhat alleviated by an ointment made by simmering prickly pear in bear's grease, which a compassionate squaw prepared for her. During this season of distress, she often wished for death, but the hope of being at some future day delivered from her cruel bondage, would support her to a patient endurance of her protracted trials. Some of the articles in her possession had been taken from her. A knife was left, which she preserved with the greatest care, and took every opportunity, when unobserved, of cutting her name on the bark of trees, in the hope that the marks might lead to her rescue.

It is supposed that this party of Indians remained a year in the northwestern part of Tennessee, at the forks of Cumberland and Tennessee Rivers, and near the junction of the Ohio with the Mississippi, afterwards passing into what is now Indiana. Several white prisoners were brought in, meanwhile, from Tennessee and Kentucky: amongst them, a man named Riddle and his two daughters, who were occasionally in Miss Nealy's company. At all times, when her health permitted, Mary was engaged in some useful occupation, never caring how laborious it might be, as her mental disquietude was thus relieved. The only employment she objected to, was the moulding of bullets, to which she was often compelled. As the journey continued, she became acquainted with a French fur-trader, whom she besought to aid her in effecting her escape. He would not listen to her entreaties, and she left him indignant at his want of humane feeling. A little conscience-stricken, perhaps, for his refusal, he brought a blanket the next day, and offered it to her; but she rejected the gift, saying that she scorned to receive any thing from a heartless wretch, who was too cowardly to give her the aid she required.

After they had passed into Michigan, where their numbers were increased by other captives, one of the females, weak from exhaustion and carrying an infant a few months old, failed to keep up with the rest, though assisted occasionally by the kind-hearted squaws. When they encamped at night, a consultation was held among the men, and it was resolved to kill the child. They had built a large fire, and when the wood had been consumed to a bed of glowing coals, one of the warriors snatched the babe from its mother's breast and threw it into the midst. It was instantly drawn out and thrown back into the arms of its distracted mother; again snatched from her and thrown into the fire, to be again drawn out; and this fiendish pastime was repeated amidst the screams of the agonized parent, and hideous yells from the savages, leaping and dancing the while with frantic gestures, till life was extinct in the little victim; when it was torn to pieces by the murderers. Scenes like this, which were not of uncommon occurrence, inspired Miss Nealy with a feeling of detestation towards the perpetrators of such outrages, which became habitual, and amounted to a vindictive hate, of which she could never wholly divest herself. She would never speak their language unless compelled by circumstances to use it, and used to say, that the only favor she ever asked of them was that she might be put to death. When in after life, a favorite granddaughter, who had been born and reared in her house, expressed a desire to wear ear-rings, and was about to purchase a pair, she persuaded her not to do so, speaking with melancholy earnestness on the subject, and saying she should never be able to look at her beloved child without pain, if decorated with ornaments which would so strongly remind her of her savage enemies.

It was Miss Nealy's lot to witness, at one time, the punishment of a young Indian and his paramour, for a crime rarely committed among the savage tribes. The criminals were bound to separate trees, and stoned to death, the white prisoners being compelled to see the execution.

Many more incidents of adventure, peril, and suffering are remembered by the family and descendants of our heroine, during her forest travel and sojourn with her wild companions. But the limits of a brief sketch permit only the record of those necessary to illustrate the experience common to too many in those fearful days of our republic. After a captivity of two years, the prisoners were taken to Detroit, where the Indians expected to receive from the British Government, payment for the scalps they had brought. The savages received much attention from the English, as important allies, while encamped in the neighborhood of the city. Mary was sent every day to the house of a French resident, to procure milk for a sick child of the chief. She saw the mistress of the house frequently, who became interested in her when she had learned her history. One morning, she told her to come on the following day; to drop her milk can outside the gate, enter the house without rapping, and proceed directly to a certain room. The poor girl had been suffering from chills and fever for several weeks. The next morning, when she was ordered to go for milk, it happened that her paroxysm of fever was upon her. In her half delirious state, revolving her plan of escape, she lingered looking for a pair of silver shoe buckles, and was struck twice by her angry master before she set out on her errand. By the time she had reached the Frenchman's gate, her senses were sufficiently restored to remember the directions of the day previous. When the Indians came in search of her, the woman of the house informed them that the girl had come to the gate, apparently in anger, had thrown down the vessel and departed, she did not know whither. On the following day men were sent by the city authorities, to whom complaint had been made by the Indians, to search the house; but no trace of the fugitive could be found. All this time, Mary lay quietly concealed in a small, dark closet, the door of which, opening into a larger one, could not be easily discovered. She occupied that room for a month, sustained by the kind care of her benefactress. An accident had nearly betrayed her one day, when, looking carelessly from the window, she was startled by seeing the face of an Indian whom she knew, and by the gleam of his eyes, saw that he had also recognized her. She hastened to inform her protectress, and implore her aid. There was no time to be lost. She was supplied immediately with boy's apparel, her hair was cut off, and she was sent, accompanied by the son of her hostess, half a mile into the city to the house of another kind-hearted Frenchwoman, who gave her shelter, and kept her concealed several weeks. Work was also procured for her from a tailor, and she was enabled to earn sufficient to clothe herself comfortably. When the fear of pursuit was over, she was removed by night to an island in the river, where she found seventeen other captives whom she had met before, in her travels through Indiana, Ohio, or Michigan; some of them having been purchased by the British authorities, some having escaped through the assistance of the French inhabitants of the city.

Our heroine remained but three weeks in this new asylum. On leaving the island, the captives were conveyed down the lakes, stopping some time at Niagara, and down the St. Lawrence River, and were landed upon the shore of Lake Champlain, where they were exchanged as prisoners of war. Before they quitted the vessel, one of the British officers endeavored to exact a promise from the company, which consisted of women, old men and boys, that they would not aid or abet the continentals against the royal government during the continuance of the war. Mrs. Spears was accustomed to relate, with much dignity and spirit, how she refused to give the pledge, and challenged the officer to go on shore with her into a thicket of bushes, where she "would cut a switch, and brush him till he would be glad to promise, on his own part, that he would never again be caught upon provincial ground." She would describe the scene with as much pride at ninety, as she could have acted in it threescore and ten years before. The others caught a portion of her spirit, and in very truth cut them switches as soon as they were on shore, daring the officer to come on, and giving three cheers for the brave young woman.

Her companions told her also that they were in expectation of seeing one of the American generals in a few days, and that when he came he would provide her with a horse and saddle. She continued her journey with this company for several days; and when the others faltered from fatigue, and were unable to proceed, she went on in the hope of finding employment among the Dutch settlers, her only companions being an old man and two boys. After a day or two of weary travel in the snow, these also gave up, and one morning left her to proceed alone. It was a sad day for her—tramping on through the snow and water in which her feet plunged at every step, and towards evening a heavy rain drenched her garments. Yet her courage did not fail, for she had now before her the hope of eventually reaching her beloved home, and felt that her success depended on herself alone.

She could not persuade herself to stop for rest till after dark, when she came up to the door of a small cabin where a cheerful light was glimmering. Very cheering was the aspect of the huge blazing logs in the ample chimney, but other comforts there were none—scarce even a morsel of bread; and not a bed could be furnished on which to lay her wearied limbs. She was, however, accustomed to hardships, and lying down on the floor with her feet to the fire, without stopping to dry her clothes, soon fell into a profound slumber. In the morning she awoke in great distress from oppression at the lungs, and unable to speak except in a whisper. The woman in the cabin, though wretchedly poor, had a kind heart, and made the suffering stranger as comfortable as she could. Miss Nealy, from her acquaintance with Indian life, had acquired a knowledge of diseases and of medicine, which now proved useful in her own case. She happened to have some medicines about her, which she directed the good woman how to prepare and administer. A severe attack of illness finally yielded to the youthful vigor of her constitution, strengthened by endurance of all kinds of hardship, but it was some weeks before she was able to travel.

In the fear of a recurrence of scurvy, from which she had previously suffered, she procured at a little settlement a few days' journey from this cabin, a small quantity of snuff and other simple remedies prescribed by a traveller, spending almost the last penny she possessed for these and a little japanned snuff-box, which she presented afterwards to the lady from whom

I received this narration. In this settlement she also learned that a farmer who lived in the vicinity intended to remove with his family in the spring to the southwestern part of Virginia; and that his wife was in want of a "help" to spin, weave, and make up men's and boys' clothing. This was good news indeed, and she lost no time in making application to be received in that capacity.

During the winter our heroine labored assiduously, doing the washing of the family and milking the cows, in addition to the other employments for which her services had been engaged; thus leaving herself not a moment of relief from toil till late bedtime, and receiving in return only fifty cents a week, and but a small part of her wages in money. When the family set out on their journey, she assisted in driving the stock, as well as in cooking and doing all kinds of work necessary in "camping out;" performing almost the entire journey on foot, and being compensated for her laborious services with only food and lodging, and such protection as the company of those she attended afforded her. Yet, throughout her life, she seemed to remember that family with warm affection, and spoke of them with gratitude; it was her first experience, since her doleful captivity, of human sympathy and home-feeling; and her generous heart overflowed towards those who gave it: her labors to serve them being esteemed as nothing in the balance.

When they reached the Susquehanna River—where she was to pay her own ferriage—such having been the agreement—she asked permission of the ferryman to paddle herself across in a small and leaky canoe lying on the shore, near by. He consented, warning her, however, that it was unsafe; but she was an excellent swimmer, and intent on saving her money, which she did, and crossed in safety. The people in the ferry-boat were less fortunate; when half way across, one of the cows jumped overboard and swam back to shore. The Dutch farmer requested Mary to return with him and bring the animal over; and she did so, getting her on board, holding her by the horn with the left hand, and thrusting the thumb and finger of her right into her nostrils; thus keeping the cow quiet for a distance of nearly a mile. A modern belle would laugh at such an instance of usefulness; but our grandmothers were more practical, and would not have felt ashamed of it. Its happy consequences will soon be seen.

When the travellers arrived at their place of destination, Mary obtained employment for a few days in a family. It happened that a farmer by the name of Spears, who lived in the neighborhood, called in, and heard the girl's romantic history. His wife wanted some one to assist her in household duties, and Miss Nealy was recommended to the place; she accepted the proposal to go at once, and, mounted behind her future father-in-law, rode to his house, where she remained some time waiting to find some party that might be going to Tennessee, for her fears of being recaptured by the Indians had grown stronger the farther she travelled westward.

We now turn to another scene in this "ower true

tale." When her family had ascertained beyond doubt that she had been captured by the Indians, they gave up all hope of ever seeing her again. They grieved as for one dead; but there was one whose sorrow was all too quickly banished; the betrothed lover of Mary, who, judging that the smiles of a new love would be the best consolation for his loss, speedily transferred his vows to another comely maiden, and was by this time on the eve of marriage. It happened about this period that Mary's brother went on business into the interior of Kentucky. On the very night of his arrival, he fell in, at a rustic tavern, with several travellers, who were relating their different adventures after supper. One of them had come all the way from Pennsylvania, and described with graphic glee the scene of the crossing of the Susquehanna by the Dutch emigrant family, the escape of the cow, and her recapture and bringing over by the heroic young woman. That girl, he added, had been a captive among the Indians, and had escaped from them. To this account young Nealy listened with aroused attention. "Did you hear the young woman's name?" he eagerly asked. "They called her Polly"—answered the stranger, "but I heard no other." "Did you observe that she was left-handed?" again the brother asked. "She certainly was"—was the reply; "I noticed it both in pulling her canoe, and in holding the cow." No farther information could be given; but this was enough. The brother had no doubt that this was indeed his long lost sister, and that her course had been directed homeward. And now, what was to be done?

He was convinced that no family would be likely to emigrate in a southwest direction in that time of peril; she had no chance of an escort to return home; and through the vast wilderness that intervened, how could an unprotected girl travel alone? He determined, therefore, himself to set out; go to the ferry on the Susquehanna, where the scene described was said to have taken place, and trace his sister thence, if possible. He set off accordingly, taking the precaution to make inquiry at every cabin, and of every person whom he met, lest he should pass her on the way. When in Virginia, he stopped one day to feed his horse, and make the usual inquiries at a farm-house, and was told that a young woman who had been in captivity among the Indians, and had recently come into the country, was living with a family six miles distant. Nealy lost not a moment; but flinging the saddle on his horse before he had tasted his corn, rode off in the direction pointed out. Before he had reached the house, he met his sister. What pen can describe that meeting! *

Mary made immediate preparations to return home, but suffered many hardships, and was exposed to many dangers on their way through the almost trackless wild. The howling of wolves, the screams of panthers, and the low growl of bears were familiar sounds in her ears; but nothing daunted her save the fearful thought of again falling into the hands of merciless savages. Even after her reunion with her family,

* This noble brother died about five years ago, at his residence near Nashville, Tennessee.

this terror so preyed on her mind that she had no peace, and her widowed mother yielded to her entreaties, and removed to a more secure home in Kentucky.

The story of Miss Nealy's return to Tennessee, and her strange adventures, was soon noised abroad, and her former lover, repenting his infidelity, came once more to prefer his claim to her favor. It may be conceived with what scorn she spurned the addresses of a man who had not only lacked the energy to attempt her rescue from the Indians, and had soon forgotten her, but who was now crowning his perfidy by the basest falsehood towards the other fair one to whom his faith was pledged.

Mary Nealy was united in marriage to George Spears, on the 27th of February, 1785, at her new home in Lincoln County, Kentucky.* After her marriage her mother returned with the rest of her family to Tennessee. Mrs. Spears and her husband continued to reside for two years near Carpenter's Station, in Lincoln County, and during the three succeeding years at or near Gray's Station, in Greene County, Kentucky. While living here, it was her custom to accompany her husband to the field, sometimes in the capacity of guard, sometimes to help him hoe the corn; and always carrying her children with her. On one occasion while thus occupied, they heard a whistle like the note of a wild turkey. One of their neighbors, an old hunter, cautioned them against following the sound, which he knew to be made by an Indian, whom he resolved to ferret out. He accordingly crept

* Date copied from Mrs. Spears' family Bible.

noiselessly along the ground, like one hunting the bird, till close to the spot whence the whistle came, when he fired, and an Indian fell.

On one occasion strange sounds were heard close to the dwelling at night, and Mrs. Spears, looking through a "chink" in the cabin, saw the shadow of a man stealthily moving around the house. She awoke her husband; he climbed the ladder to the loft, and putting his gun through an aperture in the roof, fired upon the savage. Five Indians started up and ran off; but he continued firing till the alarm was given at the fort, and aid was sent. A company of soldiers followed the trail for several miles, and judged the number of the savages to have been about fifty. While residing here, Mrs. Spears received intelligence of the murder of one of her brothers by the Indians.

Mr. Spears, who had no fear of them, was in the habit of going to the fort to try his skill in shooting at a target; and when he did not return by dusk, his wife would leave the cabin and betake herself with the children to the woods for safety, for her terror of lurking enemies whose cruelty she had so bitterly experienced, was very great. One night, having thus left her home, she was standing with her infant in her arms, under a widespreading tree, awaiting the return of her husband, when she heard the shrill note of a screech-owl directly over her head, and fell to the ground as if shot. She often described, in after life, the mortification she felt on recovering from her fright. In times of peculiar danger, she was accustomed to do sewing and washing for two young men at the fort, in return for their coming home every night with her husband, and lodging in the cabin.

On another occasion when they had reason to believe a large body of Indians was in the neighborhood, and were warned to leave the cabin without loss of time, Mrs. Spears hastily buried her dishes, and emptying out part of the feathers from her bed, put it on her horse, with such other articles of household service as she could carry, mounted, taking her child in her lap—though within two weeks of her second confinement—and assisted in driving away the stock. The alarm was given that the Indians were near and they must ride for their lives, and she urged her horse at full speed a mile and a half, with all her incumbrances. A party of soldiers was sent out from the fort to reconnoitre the enemy, and struck the trail of some forty savages, but did not venture to follow them more than a few miles. One day, a man named Fisher came from the fort to Mr. Spears' field, to bring a message to him. On his return he was pursued by Indians, and shot down and scalped in the sight of Mrs. Spears, before a gun could be brought to bear on the fierce assailants. Such incidents kept our pioneers in a continual state of suspense and dread, and during the time they were living in the fort for greater safety, their condition was but little more comfortable. Their cattle were continually driven off, and their hunters, as well as those who ventured out to till the ground, murdered by stealthy foes; so that they suffered terribly for want of provisions. While in the fort, Mrs. Spears heard of two more of her relations being killed by the Indians; five of her family in all falling victims to savage fury.

The three oldest children of Mrs. Spears were born during those years of terror, when the border settlers suffered so severely. Mr. Spears was a man of intelligence and sincere piety; he was a kind husband, and as they were blessed with health and competence, their home was a happy one. Mrs. Spears was gentle and amiable in her manners, and affectionate in her nature, with a warm and generous heart; always modest and yielding, except when sterner qualities were in requisition, when the strength and firmness of her nature were apparent. She made no attempt at any time to divest herself of early habits, in conformity to the improvement of the time, or changing fashions. A carriage was always at her disposal, yet she preferred riding on horseback when the journey was not too long; and in travelling far used a large covered farm wagon. Always charitable to the poor, and liberal to all with whom she had dealings, her industry and systematic housewifery were admirable, and not a moment of her time was ever wasted. Besides being engaged in weaving, sewing, and other domestic employments, she made salves, ointments, and decoctions continually for all the afflicted of her acquaintance. Her knowledge of medicine was made available to her friends and neighbors, and to the poor generally, gratuitously; while she accepted compensation from such as came from a distance and were able to offer it. It was a desire to do good which first induced her to undertake the most laborious duties of a physician among her own sex, medical practitioners being very scarce in that region; and her success soon made her so celebrated, that her aid was sought from every direction. One young man was sent forty or fifty miles to her for the cure of a white swelling. She became fond of practice, and continued to ride her circuit till a few months before her death.

There were some incidents in her experience, even after the cessation of Indian hostilities, which are highly illustrative. One morning her husband went out a short distance, taking his gun, and bidding her to follow him with his knife, if she heard firing. Hearing a report soon after, she ran with the knife in the direction of the sound, and heard soon after a second shot. Mr. Spears snatched the knife from her hands, and plunged it to the handle into——a monstrous bear, "which," Mrs. Spears used to say, "had in its embrace our biggest and best sow. It was some time before the sow recovered her breath, as each shot caused the bear to hug the tighter; though not a bone was broken."

Mrs. Spears was fond of high-mettled horses and was accustomed to ride a very spirited one. Her husband warned her that the animal was apt to run away; but our heroine declared she would cure the propensity, which she did one day, when the mare had run about a mile with her, by suddenly checking, so as to cause the animal to dash her head against the trunk of a beech tree by the roadside, while the fearless rider sprang off in time to save herself. At one time she was sent for in haste to attend a woman living on the opposite side of Green river, several miles distant. Her own babe was too young to leave, and she set off on horseback carrying it in her arms. Arriving at the river, she found that the ferry-boat had just pushed from shore. She called to the man to return, urging the necessity of the case, but the man replied that his load was too heavy. On this the spirited matron urged her mare into the water, swam her past the ferry-boat, reached the opposite bank first, and was in time to thank the ferryman for his humanity before his boat touched the landing. The child she carried on this occasion was accustomed to relate this anecdote, and its truth was confirmed by her old neighbors in Kentucky.

Mr. and Mrs. Spears removed with their servants—a negro boy and girl—to Illinois in 1824. Their three surviving children, all of whom had families, accompanied them. All had prospered and were comfortable in their worldly circumstances. They settled at Clarie's Grove, in Menard County. The parents were blessed in their children, and had "godliness with contentment." Mrs. Spears' solicitous care for her servants, in regard not only to bodily comfort, but moral and religious culture, equalled that she had bestowed on her own children, and it was returned by the most devoted affection and willing obedience. When the boy—Jem—became of age, his mistress gave him a liberal outfit, with liberty to depart if he chose to do so; but he preferred remaining with her. By thrifty increase of his store, Jem was enabled afterwards to purchase both his parents, who belonged to a relative of Mrs. Spears, then residing in Missouri. They were redeemed by the dutiful son, and brought to Clarie's Grove. The sympathy and aid given by Jem's mistress to this cherished project, may throw additional light on her most lovely and Christian character.

At a very advanced age—between eighty and ninety—Mrs. Spears visited her brother in Tennessee. This brother in the time of the Indian war was riding in company with her mother when she was wounded by a shot from an Indian. He killed the assailant, but while attempting to place his mother again in the saddle, received a shot from another lurking savage. A man who accompanied them helped him to mount his horse, and the party made good their escape. On her way to visit this brother, Mrs. Spears travelled in a large covered wagon, and was accompanied by her grandson, a boy about fourteen years of age. They camped out every night. During one day Mrs. Spears had noticed a horseman pass them several times, and attentively mark, as she thought, one of her best horses. Apprehensive of thievish intent, she had her bed laid that night on the ground, that her quick ear might hear the sound of approaching footsteps. In the dead silence of the night she heard the sound, and raising herself, with a loud voice demanded who was there? The intruder retired without making any answer; but in the space of an hour or two returned with the same stealthy step, which was again detected by the watchful matron. Starting up, she repeated her question, and when no reply came, charged the man with his nefarious design, and threatened punishment if he dared to come again. The thief did not seem inclined to give up his prey, but came the third time on horseback. The matron, aware of his approach, prepared herself for him, and as he came near, suddenly sprang towards him, holding a large article of dress, which she flapped in his horse's face with such a report that the animal wheeled round in affright, and bounded swiftly out of her sight. Then she was uneasy lest the rider had been thrown and killed; till by laying her ear to the ground she could hear the regular receding tramp of the horse.

Having been a widow fifteen years, Mrs. Spears died at her residence at Clarie's Grove, on the 26th January, 1852, surrounded by affectionate children and grandchildren, who still reverently cherish the memory of her virtues, and look to the example of her useful and religious life. The times of trial which nurtured such noble natures, by developing their strength, may never return in our powerful and prosperous country; yet have we all work to do in the great battle of life, and not without lasting benefit may we contemplate the character of those heroic matrons who bore so much of the burden in our struggle for Independence, and whose influence was so controlling and extensive, though unacknowledged in history, which deals only with the actions of men.

About four miles from Alton, in Madison County, stands the Monticello Female Seminary, one of the most celebrated in the Western country. It is a pleasant drive of sixteen miles from Bunker Hill, through varied scenery of prairie, oak opening, and broken country, accomplished by a carriage full of us, including the children, in little more than three hours. The light rains that marked the equinoctial had but just sufficed to lay the dust, without replenishing the numerous streams that had exhaled their being during the unprecedented drought. Every strip of timber-land had its deep dry channel, over which a bridge of logs here and there remained as if in mockery of things so evanescent as the running water which a few months since murmured beneath the overhanging foliage, and flashed in the sun between the grassy banks. Nearer the river, the country appeared more thickly settled, till at a single view the eye could take in a dozen or more farms on the extensive prairie, every farm-house garnished with its park-like plantation of trees; for hereabouts, where shade is rarely to be found, trees are set out around the humblest habitation. It is the squatter in the forest who cuts down every vestige of the wood within an arrow-shot of his dwelling—so that "the sun can shine in nicely all day long, looking so improvement like."

One could hardly find any where a country of more inviting aspect than that in the midst of which is situated the little village of Godfrey; so named after Benjamin Godfrey, a prominent citizen, who fourteen or fifteen years since, selected on his land a site for the seminary, which he built at his own expense. This building is of stone, painted a light color, one hundred and ten by forty-four feet, and four stories high, and stands in the centre of about eight acres of highly cultivated ground. There is a garden tastefully arranged, a spacious lawn in front, laid out in walks, sprinkled with arbors and summer-houses, and ornamented with flower-beds and shrubbery. From the observatory on the top of the building a magnificent view can be obtained of an extensive sweep of country on every side; the undulating prairie stretching for miles northward, with its smooth fields, its orchards and groves, and its neat homesteads; a pleasing variety of woodland, meadow, and cultivated farms in other directions, a misty height in the distance being seen on the other side of the Mississippi. The surrounding region is among the earliest settled in the State, and more than thirty years have passed since its pioneers came to till the wild prairie soil in the neighborhood.

At Jacksonville is another Female Seminary of note, and also the "Illinois Female College." This State affords a useful example to others, and it would be well if public attention were more generally directed to the establishment and support of institutions for female education, where the useful and higher branches of learning would be more effectively taught than in our flimsy, fashionable boarding-schools. It will be in vain for conventions to pass resolutions condemnatory of the public sentiment which consigns women to labor at unprofitable employments, excluding them from lucrative ones, as long as the general tone of female education is so low as it is. Some women, it is true, may be well educated enough to fill situations now appropriated by men; but the generality are deficient, and the whole sex must be concluded incapable for the fault of the majority. A late "resolution," passed at Syracuse, complained that women could not be tried by a jury of their peers. I would ask the members of that convention, which of them would be willing to be tried, if accused, by a jury of women, unless it were one "packed" with those whose education was far above the ordinary standard? The fact is no less lamentable than evident, that throughout the length and breadth of this land, with all its boasted advantages for the diffusion of knowledge, the education of women is, in general, so defective, that for all useful purposes it amounts to nothing. Even where brilliant superficial accomplishments are possessed, how frequently do we see the mind uninformed, the faculties undeveloped, the tastes uncultivated! With a better system of education, with the same advantages enjoyed by the other sex brought within the humblest means, what a change might be wrought! How many females might be saved from marriages of convenience, which in most cases lead to unhappiness, and enabled to impart such knowledge to their children, and implant such principles in their breasts betimes, as should protect them against vicious allurements, and lead to a life of integrity and usefulness.

The plan proposed by Miss Beecher, of endowing institutions in which female teachers may fill the different departments, with such salaries as would make it an object for the best qualified to seek the employment, is an excellent one. Now the disproportion between the payment of male and female instructors is excessive and most unjust. A professor may have his two or three thousand a year, for his duty of two hours a day, in a seminary of learning, while one of the other sex, as well qualified to teach the same branches, could scarcely obtain three hundred by the devotion of her whole time. The consequence is that women never take up the profession of teaching unless compelled by painful necessity. These evils might be remedied in part by the liberal endowment of institutions where women would be educated with a view to their devotion to special branches of study, and these must be under State patronage, for the want is too extensive to be supplied by individual contributions.

We spent the day and night at the residence of one of the early settlers, a mile from Monticello, and dined on the following day at the house of Dr. B——, who accompanied us in our visit to the Seminary. The little ones were very merry as we drove back to Bunker Hill, and the circle at Clay Cottage heard the narration of our adventures, including an "apple-bee," with an interest which the reader can in nowise share.

The visit of a travelling menagerie at Bunker Hill caused an excitement through the country for miles around, scarcely equalled within the recollection of the "oldest inhabitant." At an early hour the village was filled with visitors from every direction; farmers of the better class, with their neat covered carriages and buggies, or lumber wagons furnished with split-bottom chairs and boards on springs; and hordes of "suckers" from the cabins on the prairies far and near. "West Prairie," a kind of Alsatia to this region, poured forth its numbers, mail carriers left their budgets to take care of themselves, and the villagers, great and small, turned out, notwithstanding that every housewife had more than her share of company to entertain at the noonday meal; for it is a common practice to drive in wagon loads to the door of an acquaintance, and unceremoniously partake of any meal in preparation, without question as to the convenience of the person visited. A cousin of mine informed me she had twenty-two to dine with her unexpectedly on that day, six or eight arriving after she had put on her bonnet and taken her children by the hand to lead them to the exhibition. The assemblage numbered two thousand or more, and thronged the circular tent erected for the performance of the animals, so that it was difficult to find a vacant space, till the great elephant was marched round the ring to clear the circle. It was curious to observe the predominant and peculiar *Western* aspect of the multitude, a sturdy, labor-hardened look of self-reliance, an air of independent strength and will, appropriate to lords of the soil, indebted to themselves alone for their right, and intent on progress by their own might. This was observable even in the women, many of whom had infants in their arms, and were followed by two or three little ones. There was a sprinkling of the Irish physiognomy, but it bore a small proportion to the rest. It was intensely warm, and while I stood waving a huge fan for the benefit of four in our party, several requests were sent from different parts of the concourse—"to borrow that 'ere fan." The show was ended early enough for an afternoon rendezvous, but few stayed to pay visits, and the roads in every direction were lined with wagons on the return, long before sunset.

The borrowing system is in full operation in these parts; milk, cream, butter, and all articles for table use, as well as kitchen furniture, maintain a brisk circulation through the community; vegetables and fruits are regarded as common property; the thrifty resident will have applications for his garden products before they are ripe for plucking, and if disposed to be liberal, will have no chance of tasting them himself. Orchards in apple-time are alive with a dense population of boys, armed with huge baskets to carry away the fragrant treasures; what little they leave being devoured by the neighbors' pigs. The owner is often obliged to ask as a favor permission to fill two or three barrels for his own winter use, and this must be done betimes. The same "free and easy" custom of appropriation prevails in the stores, where the country people who come in to lounge and smoke away an hour or two while waiting the arrival of the mail, always help themselves to such ephemera as apples, crackers and cheese, nuts or candies, filling their pockets to beguile the journey home. On the day of the menagerie, there was a crowd of wagons and horses around every shop in the village, making approach impossible, and I noticed that several barrels of biscuit and rosy apples which had been displayed, disappeared mysteriously before evening, while I ascertained by inquiry that the people never bought such things by the small quantity. As soon as the letter-bag is opened every curious farmer who has a mind, examines the letters, holding them to the light, and throwing them on the counter when his curiosity is satisfied.

Another prominent feature in country life in this State, and almost every where at the West, is the difficulty in obtaining "help" in domestic service. The daughters of the poorer class of farmers are needed at home, and have no inducement to live out beyond the procuring a little extra clothing occasionally by a few weeks' labor, as a great favor, with some neighbor able to hire; the Irish and Germans who emigrate to the country can obtain land on easy terms, and have a home of their own as speedily as they please; and most of them are too much in love with the independence they see in all around them, to be willing to remain long in a subordinate condition. The consequence is, that the wives of most of the substantial freeholders are obliged to do without servants altogether; and when they can be obtained, which is always with extreme difficulty, they are, as a rule, ignorant and inefficient. They have learned, too, to be jealous to a degree of any assumption of superiority on the part of their employers; for example, the indignity of not being invited to the family table, is deeply resented; or if the girl herself fail to notice the infringement on her dignity, her companions and acquaintances will give her no peace till it is complained of, and her injured feelings are propitiated. Such housewives as have been fortunate enough to procure tolerable help—it is literally *help*, for every domestic expects her mistress to work with her, and perform the most difficult portion of the labor—live in continual fear of giving offence to those employed, and thereby provoking them to go away. The awe with which the Venetian, in the days of the Secret Inquisition, was accustomed to whisper of "those above," was hardly deeper than that expressed in the subdued, fearful tone with which, glancing around to see that walls have not ears, the Western lady ventures to speak of her hired damsel. Insolence must be borne submissively, and she dares not reprove for a fault even of ignorance. The hard experience she has too frequently to undergo, in performing herself the whole labor of her household, burdened also in most cases with the care of a young family, has taught her to value highly the most imperfect assistance, and to make sacrifices of her own feelings to procure and retain it. This state of things, I am told, is the most serious drawback on comfort in living at the West; it is an evil bitterly felt, and likely to prevent, instead of fostering, the growth of kindly feeling between the different classes of settlers.

XIII.

IF it be an era in one's life to be for the first time

> "Where the wild will of Mississippi's tide
> Has dashed him on the sawyer——"

the first sight of the boiling, turbid Missouri, and the mingling of its waters with those of the Father of Rivers, is not less so. Here the dark, clear stream which has swept through its vast primeval solitudes thousands of miles southward, suddenly loses its pure appearance, and, as if angry at the change, pursues its way with accelerated rapidity, with current deep and resistless, gathering strength as it sweeps onward to the ocean that receives its mighty tribute.

On the morning of the 28th September, I left Bunker Hill, accompanied by three of the cousins who bear my name, arrived at the house of Rev. Mr. L., in Middle Alton, about noon, and in the afternoon drove to the "Lower Town." One of the finest views to be had of the winding Mississippi, is presented from the heights of Alton. Sad it was to see the noble river so shorn of its fair proportions—a waste of sand on either side, the shrunken stream pursuing its course with diminished speed in the midst. One would think the term "dusty rivers" a figure of speech; yet the course of this may often be tracked by the clouds of dust raised by the wind from the sandbanks in the channel exposed at low water.

The next morning, leaving the house of our venerable relation, we drove to the levee a little before nine. The town of Alton, picturesquely situated on the heights, showed very imposingly from the river for many miles down. The Missouri at its mouth was much narrower than I expected; and a passenger observed that he had ascended it for three thousand miles, and found it of the same or greater width. The sand-wastes on either side showed that we saw no more than half the stream as it usually is. Its muddy waters, as they poured into the Mississippi, formed a contrast with the clear stream, the line of division being perfectly defined; gradually it encroached further and further, till the purer portion was driven into narrow limits on the eastern side, which it maintains as its own even to St. Louis. The quality of this muddiness is remarkable, and the thickest is brought to the surface by the whirlpools and eddies; so that it seems an opaque, swiftly moving mass, on which the shadow of the line of curling smoke looks like a clear rift between two shifting bodies of yellow sand. The gully-like banks, which are overflowed at high water, show the deposits of sand four or five feet deep on the natural soil, and are covered with a growth of stunted willows. The cotton-wood that grows thickly on the alluvial bottoms, is said to increase with almost tropical rapidity, and is used for steamboat firewood. The shallowness of the water is seen in the wake the boat leaves on the bosom of the angry giant; and a snag here and there reveals the terror of the rivermen of the West.

The view of the "Mound City," as St. Louis is called, is extremely fine. Without preparation in villas or villages, you see on the right, throned like a queen, the forest-girdled mart of merchandise and business—the New-York of the West. Its steeples and domes, its ranges of buildings rising one above another, its levee thronged with carts and wagons and piled with merchandise, and its crowded streets, form a strange contrast to the wild and romantic view further down the river, with the blue hills bounding the sight. The long range of steamboats—their forest of tall pipes lining the shore for miles, discloses the secret of this commercial prosperity and activity. "Not a squatter builds his cabin on the Yellow Stone or the Platte; not a hunter or trapper takes his prey on all the broad lands that skirt the base of the Rocky Mountains, but he is contributing to the growth of this emporium." The streets of the city are regularly laid out, well built up, and tolerably cleanly. The number of trees, and the dull, stained appearance of the brick buildings, give it the aspect of a Southern city, and there is a Southern twang in the speech of its fair inhabitants. The Planter's House, centrally situated in the goodliest part of the city, is pronounced the bestby the universal suffrage of citizens and visitors.

Some members of a highly respectable family residing in this hotel, were said to have been, for the last three or four months, participants and witnesses of many marvels in the way of "spiritual manifestations." The fame of these mysterious appearances had gone over the whole city, and produced no little excitement on the subject, and the sensation had extended to neighboring towns.

My cousin and I were invited one evening to witness some of the phenomena; but saw nothing convincing. Viewing them, if they really exist, simply as dependent on the established laws of nature, a better knowledge of which might be made available to useful purposes, I should think the subject worth the investigation of philosophical minds. If proved, on the other hand, to be produced by supernatural agency, no one who acknowledges the authority of the Bible will pay attention to them, or withhold his censure. Intercourse with "familiar spirits" was punished with death under the Mosaic laws; it may fairly be considered as included in the "sorcery" denounced in the New Testament; and every such unhallowed attempt, by unhallowed means, to obtain knowledge not revealed in the Book of Truth, must lead to evil results.

The style of dress in vogue among the ladies appears to be the most splendid, without much regard to season. When New-York dames would wear barêges and muslins, those of St. Louis prefer rich silks, brocades, etc. One afternoon a friend conducted me to the top of the Court-House, from which a magnificent view is obtained. The course of the Mississippi may be seen with its yellow sand-banks and wide bordering of alluvial bottom, and far to the east one or two small lakes are visible, and a range of bluffs forms the boundary of the waters at an unusual flood.

One of the curiosities of the place, and a fair specimen of the class of steamers preparing to accommodate the increase of travel to and from New-Orleans, was the "Charles Belcher," waiting a rise in the waters to go out. Her length "from stem to stern" is two hundred and ninety feet, her width seventy-two, and her dining and ladies' cabins are as splendid as rich upholstery and painting can make them. The superb carpets are soft as velvet, and the divans, couches and easy chairs are as luxurious. The butler's and kitchen apartments are a curiosity for convenience and adaptation, as is the steerage, furnished with state-rooms for sixty-four persons, where emigrant families, performing the journey for two dollars, can be as secluded as in the upper cabins for twenty-five. There are state-rooms above for one hundred and forty persons, and more can be taken in an emergency. The crowning glory of the boat is her bath-rooms, which are elegantly fitted up and provided with hot and cold water and shower baths. When we remarked that these were an unspeakable convenience, the captain said he would wager that they would be scarcely used during the season, and mentioned that the commander of one of the Louisville packets which had bath-rooms, had assured him that no lady and only four gentlemen had ever taken a bath on board since the boat had been built. This confirms what I have already observed of the *hydrophobia* common among American travellers.

The want of punctuality in the starting and arrival of boats we have already had occasion to remark. Here, as well as further up the river, it is common to advertise an intended departure several hours and even days in advance of the real time, and passengers who have gone on board with the expectation of being off directly, often have to wait till their patience is exhausted. "How soon does the boat leave?" asked one in a hurry of a captain of a steamer going to New-Orleans. "In five minutes," was the brisk reply. "I am sorry for that," rejoined the other, "as I hoped to take passage with you; I cannot go before to-morrow." "All right," responded the official, "we shall not get off till the day after." Even the packets which ply every day up and down the river, often vary some hours from their appointed time. In view of this custom, it was a thunder-stroke to find the new steamboat "Cornelia," in which our party expected to go up the river, had started just one minute *before* her time, carrying off the luggage previously sent on board. The telegraph, the usual resort in such cases, conveyed directions to Mr. Bliss, the proprietor of the Franklin House in Alton, who forthwith secured and preserved it. The swift and beautiful Altona brought us up in the evening, in company with a bridal party, and all found a cheerful welcome and a brilliant reception at the Franklin.

The cars for Springfield leave Alton at eleven o'clock in the morning, giving time for the arrival of the boat from St. Louis. This new railroad is in excellent order, and provided with elegant and commodious cars. We had little more than an hour's travel before the train stopped at a station called Shipman, where we had expected to find the germ of a village, but we looked in vain for any inhabited dwelling. In three minutes the cars had rolled away in thunder, leaving us—two ladies and a child—somewhat surprised to find ourselves beside our pile of luggage, on the wide, waste prairie—an unfinished tank-house on one side, an empty building on the other. Seeing an old man at work not far off, I went to ask information; but he was deaf as the post he was planting. My companion had better luck with a farmer who chanced to pass within sight, and who, as soon as he learned our plight, went to "gear up"—offering to take us in his farm-wagon wherever we would. A mile distant stood the residence of a friend, Captain G——, and we were soon set down, luggage and all, before his gate—our courteous farmer, with true Western kindliness, refusing to accept any reward for his trouble in bringing us. The traveller in the West continually meets with such instances of disinterested kindness, proffered wherever it is needed, without the least ostentation.

Captain G—— is one of the pioneers of this section, and his house stands on the open prairie, embowered in a plantation of shade-trees, his broad, rich fields, under the best cultivation, presenting the ideal of an excellent farm. After a few hours spent pleasantly with his charming daughters, his carriage was ready to convey us to Bunker Hill, where our arrival was warmly welcomed by affectionate relatives.

On the sixth of October we bade adieu to this pleasant village and its inhabitants, and taking the cars at Shipman, in three or four hours were in Springfield, the capital of Illinois. This town, containing about seven thousand inhabitants, is regularly laid out on the bosom of an extensive prairie, and occupies space enough for a large city. The streets are straight and broad, but the houses generally low, small, and scattered. There are raised sidewalks and crossings, quite necessary in the condition of the unpaved streets after a rain—the thick black mud being absolutely terrific to the inexperienced pedestrian. The capitol and public buildings around the central square are solid and imposing. There are several hotels, of which the City Hotel is the most popular, and enjoys a wide reputation for the excellence of its table. The proprietor, Mr. Johnson, is a genuine specimen of the Western landlord, enterprising, liberal, and energetic in his superintendence of every department. The occurrence of a masonic celebration, and a projected fair, had brought a large concourse of country people to the place, and at every meal both stratagem and force were necessary to guard the quiet inmates of the house from the rush of a tumultuous crowd, every man of which scrambled in and devoured what was before him, as if life, with all its blessings, depended on his dispatching the repast in two minutes and three quarters.

A trunk belonging to me was here discovered to

be out of repair, and the town was traversed in a vain search for a locksmith. A hardware storekeeper sent a couple of boys in the evening to mend it, who, on being offered payment, declined it, saying that "the boss had forbidden them to receive any thing; it was an accident, &c."—another instance of the unostentatious courtesy so common in the country. Some one has asked a definition of the differences between Southern and Western chivalry. A chief one is this: at the South, this kindly and liberal spirit is peculiar to the more cultivated classes of society; the lower—I mean white people—are degraded and selfish, with few exceptions. The southern *gentleman* will throw open his house to the traveller, and entertain him with liberal hospitality; the poor "sandhiller" or "sucker" is farther removed than the negro from such a footing of sociability, and proffers no civilities. At the West, on the other hand, the spirit of freedom and independence is universally diffused, and overflows in cordial good will towards the stranger; the laborer without a coat will tender you, if you stand in need, the hospitalities of his mud cabin with as frank a grace as if he were lord of a manor, and scorn the thought of remuneration.

There is a stage running from Springfield to Peoria, but the necessity of night travelling, and the horrible state of the roads, made this seem a formidable undertaking. The knowledge that a lady dreaded this seventy miles' journey, brought the liberal offer of a private carriage, tendered gratuitously for the trip, through Mr. Johnson, which was declined, of course, but with a grateful memory of the kindness. We took the morning train westward to Naples, to meet the boats ascending the Illinois River. This railroad passes, like the other, through a continuous extent of prairie, varied now and then by a strip of timber, with its running stream. By this time, I must own to being weary of prairiedom; those vast undulating plains look beautiful when driving rapidly over them, or when alternated with forest; but there is something depressing in an unvaried succession of the same monotonous features of scenery, and I longed already for the exhilarating aspect of wooded mountain, lake and river.

Jacksonville, a flourishing town upon this route, is noted for its Female Seminary and College. It is about half as large as Springfield, and is a very pretty place. Passing on, we found less uncultivated prairie, and considerable tracts of marsh land. Naples, fifteen miles from Jacksonville, is a small place lying on the Illinois River, showing a number of scattered, dirty houses, looking dreary enough in the gray, rainy atmosphere, and the waste of dark, deep mud in which they stand; it might pass, in truth, for the capital of the uninhabitable globe! The river view, nevertheless, with its wooded shores and islands, is a fine one. The almost desert solitude of the hotel contrasted oddly enough with the scene of the previous day; we could get sight of neither landlord nor servants, and while waiting for the boat, the hours passed wearily. When evening came with no nearer prospect of relief, we hailed the first appearance of a woman, who appeared to be the landlady, and asked to be shown to sleeping apartments. She led the way to *one* very scantily furnished with a single chair and narrow bed, and when it was submitted that two ladies could not well occupy such premises together, she replied, with much tartness, that she had never heard of such fastidiousness, and asked my companion if she did not feel offended by my unwillingness to share a bed with her? My audacity being followed by a timid request for water, the woman thrust her hand into the pitcher, and having ascertained that there was nearly a pint (enough for any two reasonable persons), she darted a fierce look, as much as to say, "Dare you jest with me?" which deprived me of courage to venture a suggestion that another towel might be desirable. A request for clean sheets would in all likelihood have been followed by a buffet; the more prudent course, therefore, was to submit quietly. The night passed in restless expectation of the steamboat bell; and as the gray dawn was breaking, its welcome sound broke on the humid air, followed by a vigorous knock at the door, and the announcement that the boat was ready at the wharf. It was with gladdened hearts that we found ourselves on board the "Summit," and ploughing our way up the river at the very moderate rate necessary at the low stage of water. The most expeditious, easiest, and cheapest route from St. Louis to Chicago, is by these packets up the Illinois River. At an ordinary stage of water, the trip is made in two days to La Salle, whence a railway communication is now complete to Chicago.

The shores of the Illinois are generally flat and covered with woods frequently tall and luxuriant as the oak groves of Michigan. The steep banks, seven or eight feet above the present level of the water, show their course at high flood. The site of Beardstown is flat; the town of Pekin occupies ground much higher, and cannot be seen to advantage from the river. A large, brick hotel, surmounted by a tower-like observatory, was invitingly conspicuous, and we longed to obtain the view that must be commanded from such a height; but the rain forbade any attempt to walk up the banks to the building.

Peoria is a large and handsome town, with about seven thousand inhabitants, and seems to be a place of active business, its situation giving it every advantage for growth and prosperity. The ground ascends in a gentle slope from the river to a considerable elevation, the town lying on the slope and crowning the height. The Illinois here expands into a lake seventeen miles in length, and from half a mile to a mile and a half wide. The banks are bold and in some places precipitous, and one point, where a massive range of rock rises from the stream as it takes a bend, is very romantic. A stationary light here warns night voyagers of peril. The scenery becomes more varied as we proceed; hills are seen in the distance, and shadowy groves of stately trees, beginning to put on the gorgeous livery of autumn, were a feast for the lover of nature's beauty.

The town of Peru is situated on the top of a bluff, reached by a steep ascent from the river. La Salle, a mile or so distant, also occupies an elevated site. The mud was formidable, but we succeeded in gaining the height, which commands an extensive view of the river, marsh-land, and surrounding country. Many of the passengers waited on board the "Summit" for the evening packet to Chicago, and an excellent dinner was prepared for them all, for which payment was refused; the good captain seemed to take pleasure in hospitably entertaining them, and that without the least ostentation of liberality, but as a matter of course. The packet boat was a miniature craft, but scrupulously clean. It was curious to see how every square inch of it was put to use, and the way the passengers were obliged to "stand around," while the shelves were put up for their sleeping accommodation, was "a caution." We reached Chicago in the afternoon, and after a pleasant evening spent at Judge W——'s, took places for a night ride in the spacious cars of the Michigan Central Railroad.

We found the climate of the lakes rather bracing after the soft temperature of Southern Illinois. Yet emigration northward was still rife; an acquaintance had just set off to locate land in Minnesota; and it was with a feeling of envy that we heard of the rivers of the territory being in navigable order, affording opportunities for excursions impossible to us in the heats of August.

We were told afterwards that the descriptive letters published in the Tribune, had induced hundreds to visit those regions. They found, doubtless, that the half had not been told them. How could it be in so brief a sojourn? For the information of those who have solicited it, I would add, that the most comfortable route from New-York is by the Albany and Buffalo Railroad, and Michigan Central Railroad to Chicago; thence to Galena and up the Mississippi; and that the expense is from twenty-five to twenty-eight dollars from the city of New-York to St. Paul.

XIV.

DURING the last season the talk of fashionable tourists in Ohio and Michigan, was chiefly of the magnificent scenery and bracing climate of Lake Superior. Every summer will bring numbers of settlers, and it will not be long before thriving towns will take the place of the new settlements embraced in the arms of the primeval forest. The early history of this portion of our country has singular romance. More than two hundred years ago, the Jesuits of Canada first took steps to explore the country bordering the North American Lakes, under the auspices of Count Frontenac. In 1641, Raymfault and Jaques went in a bark canoe to Saut Ste. Marie, where they found Indian villages with a considerable number of inhabitants, the abundance of whitefish having made this the chosen resort of the Chippewas for centuries. They here heard of the lake beyond, and of grassy plains westward, where ran herds of deer and buffaloes, and where dwelt the warlike Sioux. In 1660, René Mesnard, in his canoe, reached the head of Keweenaw Bay, which he called St. Teresa, and was lost in the woods. Claude Allouez, six years later, entered this lake, then sacrificed to as a divinity by the savages, and landed at Chaquamegon (La Pointe), where he built a chapel and lived two years; in the mean time visiting Fond du Lac, where he heard of the Mississippi. La Hontan called this region "the fag-end of the world," and the lake was described by him as "an ocean in a storm sculptured in granite," so striking was the aspect of its towering rocks, deep ravines and giant crags, seemingly wrenched from their places by some violent convulsion of nature. About this time the southern shore of Superior, toward its western extremity, was the central region of Indian influence and intelligence. Here was the seat of power for the Chippewas; and here, tradition says, was burning that sacred fire whose extinction foretold some great calamity for the nation. The ceremonies attending its preservation by appointed guardians, are said to be remembered in Indian tradition.

The scenery along Lake Erie differs entirely from that on the Atlantic frontier. Passing up Detroit River, the view of the city and islands sleeping calmly on the waters, with the sunlit river and the distant expansion into Lake St. Clair, form a lovely picture. The city is lost behind the woods as you enter on the broad calm sheet of this fairy lake, passing, in a few hours, into St. Clair River, where the character of the scenery changes, losing its aspect of cultivation and populous life, but gaining in interest as the shores become bolder, the islands more thickly wooded, and the clustering thickets on the banks darker and more impervious. Approaching Lake Huron, the scenery grows still wilder; uplands partially cultivated rise from the river, and further back lies a line of dense forest; here and there is an island with clumps of trees and marshy shore, and you will continue to admire the brilliant shades of purple and green peculiar to these waters. Hereabouts is seen a Methodist missionary station on the British side, its white chapel and neat houses embowered in trees, and set off by the foil of an ancient wind-mill overgrown with creepers; at intervals an Indian wigwam appears, and now and then a bark canoe shooting out from the shelter of bushes, or moored on the beach, with its load of baskets, blankets, children, and squaws, in their coarse, dark clothing.

At the foot of Lake Huron, Fort Gratiot, compact against a ground of woods, with its white pickets, barracks, and tall flag-staff, commands the entrance into the upper lakes. The headlands and point with its light-house, the islands in the distance, and the long sweep of Lake Huron, complete the picture. The alluvial shore on the left is covered with pine, poplar, beech, hemlock, etc., skirted with a wide beach of sand. White Rock is said to have been an ancient place of Indian sacrifice, and is still consecrated by their superstition. It was early in the morning when we lay among the green islands of Thunder Bay—some partly covered with ragged foliage, the light-house and a few neat dwellings prominent on the nearest bank, and the long sandy shores sprinkled with fishers' huts and shanties. A crimson line on the edge of the horizon grew brighter, and presently the great sun lifted himself from the bosom of the deep, sending a radiant flush over the waste of waves and the woods on the distant isles.

The Island of Mackinaw has been called "the diadem on the brow of the North Western lakes," and its historical associations are extremely interesting. Its highest elevation is about three hundred feet above the level of the lake. From the water a fine view is presented of the old trading town, the heights with their straggling growth of trees, and the white walls and buildings of the fort. The rampart-like shore is rugged and inaccessible; and in sailing round the island, the shadows of overhanging cliffs, the masses of fallen rock, the deep caves, towering arches, and rock-based columns, with green isles dotting the crescent bay, and the straits and view of Lake Michigan in the distance, present scenes of grandeur and beauty. This is the classic ground of Indian mythology. The great curiosity of the island is the celebrated Arched Rock, a natural bridge thrown over the precipice, its grand arch overstriding fragments of rock heaped in the wildest confusion, and supported by gigantic abutments rising a hundred and forty feet from the water. The Sugarloaf Rock, a natural cone rising thirty feet from the hill, and the Skull Rock, a lofty, insulated mass, with a cavern at its base, are also noticed by visitors.

St. Mary's River is the paradise of beautiful islands, thousands of which lie in its different channels; the soft line of shore and drooping foliage and rocky headlands are doubled in the clear mirror, and now a bold shore dark with overhanging woods, appears; now you pass between islands fringed with evergreens, or alongside rocky uplands crowned with a straggling forest growth; shooting across smooth bays or along narrow straits, where abrupt turnings disclose new views of the wild and beautiful; the hills swelling gradually into loftier heights, till the Granite mountains rival in startling beauty, the higher range at the base of which the lordly Hudson takes his way. A bright sheet, called "Echo Lake," lies embosomed among rugged heights in the distance. The river banks and island shores showed, in 1851, rough clearings at intervals, with here and there a missionary station, an Indian encampment, a log hut, or pioneer cabin. In the dark impenetrable woods, the tall pines, firs, spruce, and tamarac mingle their sombre green with trees of deciduous foliage, giving a rich variety to the forest verdure.

A few more windings among the fairy isles, and "the Saut" is in view on the left shore, the tall pickets and block houses of its fort conspicuous; its neat white houses and stores below, and on the right the foaming rapids. On the point, covered with huge boulders, is a small cluster of Chippewa wigwams, the occupants of which live by fishing. If it is not the hour for sport, the men may be seen lying on their mats outside, or mending their nets, or weaving mats, or smoking with the placid enjoyment of the "dolce far niente," remarkable in the race. The interior of the wigwams shows a primitive life; the ground is strewn with hemlock boughs by way of carpet, the fire built in the centre, and the kettle over it, hanging from a horizontal pole supported by two cross-poles—containing fish or other materials for the evening repast. Around the sides is a platform two or three feet broad, raised a few inches from the ground, and spread with mats, quilts, and various articles of clothing, serving the savages for seats and beds, their feet stretched to the fire as they lie in a circle at night. In the corners are swung the pappooses in their tiny bark hammocks, or strapped to the boards on which their mammas usually carry them; their nooks shared by pet domestic fowls, dogs, or some tamed bird or animal of the forest. The spaces around the bark walls are strung with dried fruits, roots, and every variety of utensil or apparel, all well cured by the smoke, not more than half of which finds its way through the aperture in the roof. These wigwams, built in an hour or two, are the habitations of Chippewa families in the summer; in the winter they retire to log huts in the interior. Some of them are picturesquely located on the islands scattered among the rapids, on the rocky shore of which, about sunset, the squaws may be seen cleaning the whitefish just caught. I persuaded a chief whose cabin stands at the foot of the rapids to take me in his canoe. Away darted the light birchen craft into the very midst of the angry whitecaps, dexterously avoiding the rocks; the Indian in the stern directing its course with a paddle, while the one standing in the bow used a light setting-pole to push the bark up the sweeping current. Presently the fish are seen struggling to force their way up; the fisherman drops his pole quickly, and seizing his scoop-net, which is fastened to the end of another, drops it in the water a few feet ahead, and while the canoe runs back, sweeping downward, he captures the unwary prey; sometimes lifting several at once into the canoe.

A still more exciting adventure is going over the rapids in a canoe. Starting from the foot with Indian or French boatmen, the bark canoe is pushed up the swift current, winding its way among the foam-lashed boulders in the midst of the bounding, rushing, roaring waters, dazzling the eyes with the gleam of sunshine on their snowy crests, and stunning the ear with the voice of many surges. The slightest failure of strength or skill on the part of the boatmen would be the destruction of the vessel and its voyagers; but propelled by experienced hands, the feather-light craft leaps upward and onward, spurning the whirling eddies, and quivering on the foaming billows, till the last shoot is passed and it floats on the calm surface where the river bends its glassy breast to take the first leap. Turning as by an instinctive impulse, the canoe enters the deeper channel, where the heavier current sweeps furiously downward over buried rocks. By successive leaps, bounding over the billows flung back by the mighty rush of the waters, the bark is swept along with breathless speed, estimated by the rapidity with which it flies past the shores and rocky islets, and the moment of time in which the descent of three quarters of a mile is gone over.

In the village of Saut Ste. Marie there are two principal hotels and several churches. Sermons are frequently preached at the Mission to the Indians through the aid of an interpreter, though a large proportion of the savages are Catholics. The interruption of the rapid cuts off Lake Superior from continuous navigation; the portage is about three quarters of a mile, and is traversed by a railroad over which vessels and freight are conveyed.

The Alpine scenery of Lake Superior has been admired by many visitors, and its remarkable coast described by several geologists, but it has been associated chiefly with the mineral wealth of the country on its borders. To the mere rambler, until recently, it has loomed afar off as an unknown region, no white sail seen on its vast expanse; the snowy seagull alone, starting from her nest on some rocky isle, wheeled over its surface, or the canoe of the savage darted from its sheltered coves; its shores one unbroken forest, and the imagination of Indian mythology appropriating its shadowy islands for an Elysium of rest. The pass by which its waters are poured into St. Mary's River is guarded by lofty and precipitous bluffs on either side, covered with a growth of tall pines—these peaks, like the pillars of Hercules, forming a grand entrance into the lake. On the north the bold range of "Gros Cape" may be seen; on the south the promontory of Cape Iroquois, noted in ancient tradition as the locality of an Indian battle. The outlet of the lake extends several miles, and is sprinkled with green and lovely islands, around whose long, pebbly shores the vessel wound, passing numerous bays and indentations where slumber bright islets, and in the distance the conical peaks beyond Whitefish Point, a bleak, sandy peninsula, extend far into the waters. Wagishkee, familiarly Waishkee Bay, was named after a chief who cultivated fields on its borders.

The great sand-dunes of this lake, called Grandes Sables, have attracted attention as unique objects of American scenery. These form a range for some four miles, of vast heaps of sand-drift, rising like a lofty structure of marble to the height of two hundred and fifty or three hundred feet, their summits capped with loose drifts. No tree or shrub grows on the face of this precipice, and only a few scanty evergreens here and there overtop the bleak and denuded heights. Mr. Schoolcraft says these sandcliffs were imagined by Indian superstition to be a vast palace inhabited by powerful spirits or necromancers, who had only to thrust their hands through the windows to catch fish. The savages also pointed out on the sands the tracks of their fairies. Ascending the face of the precipice, a singular and imposing view is obtained from the summit. For many miles extends the waste of sand, an herbless desert; a "northern Sahara," rising into lofty cones, sweeping in graceful curves, hurled into eddying hollows, or spread out in broad valleys. The tops of half buried pines are seen here and there, barkless and ragged, and worn by whirling drifts, like the columns of some ancient temple. The surface of the sand is hard as a floor, and strewn with pebbles polished by attrition. Two miles from the coast, behind this desert tract, timber is found, and you may see a small lake far above the level of Superior, its wild and sylvan shores adorned with a rich growth of oaks and maple on one side, while the dunes of shifting sand stretch away on the other in a leafless waste, like immense snow drifts, in the midst of which the traveller seems walking over the undulating billows of ocean swelling to vast height, or looks down into deep basins. The scene has been likened to a storm among the Alps.

Grand Island, extensive and rock-bound, next appears, and the scenery becomes more varied, the bold shores rising to hills wooded with a thick growth of beech, birch and maple, mingled with the spruce, and conical fir trees. A story current hereabouts, of a Chippewa war party, may illustrate Indian devotion. Thirteen warriors suddenly encountered a party of Sioux ten times their number. The latter were inclined to a truce, but the Chippewas insisted on fighting, and were killed, after having slain twice as many of their enemies; the youngest of them, who had been directed to stand on a neighboring height, see the result, and carry the news to their tribe, being the only survivor.

The world may fairly be challenged for so magnificent a display of elevated coast, with such varied forms of architectural ruins bathing their massive and columnar fronts in the clear waters, as is presented in the Pictured Rocks. For some ten miles along the shore, these towering masses of sandstone rise in startling grandeur from the lake, sometimes to the height of three hundred feet, their surfaces exhibiting a gorgeous coloring of various hues, and forming an unrivalled panorama of precipices and caverns, majestic arches, towers, columns, Doric temples, and burgs rivalling those of the Rhine; the tufts of dark foliage adding to the wild effect, and the whole scene glowing with brilliant tints like the hues of sunset, or the gorgeous illumination of some work of art. "Le Portail" is the entrance to a large cavern in the most prominent headland in the range. From the mouth of this vast orifice the echo of the hoarse waters, as they roll into its jaws, is sent back like the roar of a volcano. No arched gateway was ever constructed in such massive proportions. Entering the dim recesses of the cavern by a winding passage, a few hundred feet, the visitor is within a rotunda awful in grandeur; the grim and massive walls, the lofty stone ceiling supported by pillars sculptured by the hand of nature in rude magnificence, the gigantic archway, and the floor of clear deep water, form a scene to which no artist's pencil could do justice. The light from the entrance, softened in the cavern to a dim twilight, is reflected from a reef of pebbles at the extremity of one of the deepest and darkest passages leading to a wide semi-circular curve of shore, where the walls have been undermined and have fallen into the lake in ruinous masses. The boat may pass out of the cavern by another entrance than the main one.

Here and there a silver thread of a waterfall flings itself from the summit of the cliff at one bound into the lake, or a broader cascade gushes from the rock, its snowy foam contrasting with the rich colors of the beetling rocks. At one point, half-way up, is a natural chapel of rock, the pillars of which seem finely sculptured and are wreathed with moss and foliage; it is about thirty feet in height, the arch fifteen. It is said that service has been performed in this primitive sanctuary; and that some Indians were there converted to Christianity by the preaching of a missionary. "Monument Rock," with its mossgrown pillars, towers conspicuous, bordered by a cascade springing in two bounds to the water; another monument half embedded in foliage is passed, and the magnificent scene begins to fade from the view.

All along the shore of the lake, islets of moss-covered granite, or fringed with pines, starting abruptly from the deep, are a remarkable feature. Sometimes a chain of them extends far out from a promontory. Granite Point is a bluff two hundred feet high, rising from the lake, and connected with the main land by a neck of sandstone and a cluster of rocky islands. Keweena Point is described as a beautiful spot. The shore is wooded with pine, cedar, aspen and spruce to the water's edge: it is cut into small bays and broken and projecting precipices; huge masses of rock are lying out in the lake, and high, conical mountains appear in the distance. Waterfalls are leaping down from the wooded cliffs, and there are green and lovely recesses, in which has been found literally "the rose without the thorn." The Indians have a tradition, that a party passing round this point and approaching Beaver Island, were terrified by the apparition of a gigantic female form; and for a long time no savage could be prevailed on to trespass on the interdicted region. Manitou Island is said also to be haunted by a demon. Within view of this are the Marquette Iron Works. At Carp River several small rocky islands rise abruptly from the lake, each crowned with its growth of evergreens, a safe home for the wild seabirds that are skimming the wave in all directions; to the left is the range of Iron Mountains, the crest of some veiled by clouds.

The view from Totosh or Breast Mountain, is described by Schoolcraft as magnificent. In front is the boundless expanse of the lake, with its archipelago of islands and peninsulas; eastward appear the white cliffs of Grand Island and the Pictured Rocks; westward the coast as far as the Huron Islands, embracing a succession of peninsulas surmounted by cliffs, the outline of each growing fainter in the distance; southward a sea of granite cones filling up the vista as far as the eye can reach. At Copper Harbor, Fort Wilkins is visible from the water, its flag overtopping the foliage; near it lies a beautiful lake two hundred feet above the level of Superior, shadowed by a grove of dark evergreens and surrounded by conical mountains. The loveliest spot on the shore is Eagle Harbor, a "quiet, spirit-stealing nook," with its bright bijou of a bay, light-house, rocky islets, and forest-circled curve, its smooth white shore, its groves of pine, cedar, spruce and tamarac, with here and there an Indian lodge; its rustic settlement, its winding stream and picturesque woods; the fir-crowned mountains beyond, with the buried wealth of their copper mines, and the misty outline of Porcupine Mountains extending far out in the lake. These mountains are said to be over thirteen hundred feet in height, and the Huron Mountains are nearly as lofty. The valley of Eagle River is bounded by abrupt overhanging cliffs, some several hundred feet high, and the rock-bound coast stretches miles onward. Two miles south of the lake, among the Porcupine Mountains, is a gorge said to be five hundred feet deep, with a small lake cradled in its depths, in the clear waters of which gloomy evergreens are reflected. This picturesque sheet of water is the source of Carp River.

The scenery of the whole shore from Whitefish Point to the Isles of the Apostles, is of this diversified character; unbroken forests in which the evergreens of the North mingle their dark verdure, small recent clearings at long intervals, the smoke of distant mines curling above the woods upon the mountains; the range of rocky highlands with broken, precipitous sides; deep bays, unsunned streams, promontories stretching miles into the water, cliffs upreared as gigantic buttresses against the roaring waves, wooded islets starting from the deep, the rugged outline of rock inland, and lofty mountains covered with their ancient garniture of woods; such are the general features of the country—with the addition of the keen, invigorating air, the waters crystal clear, the brilliant blue of heaven and the northern lights so vivid that twilight lingers till midnight. The forests of cedar and spruce on the rocky shores of Isle Royale, with their dark green boughs interlaced and wreathed with festoons of moss, are fine specimens of the growth of these northern woods. But little justice can be done by description to the varied and sublime scenery of this inland sea; it is of itself well worth a tour of observation from the farthest part of the continent.

La Pointe, an ancient post, formerly the headquarters of the fur-trading company, is on the end of Madeline Island. It is rightly named, for it seems the extreme point of the civilized globe, and might have been copied in Hogarth's picture of the world's end. The air of vigorous life belonging to the new settlements is wholly wanting here; every thing looks old and worn out; the tumble down pickets that formerly inclosed the settlement, its ruined fort, its range of dilapidated dwellings, the stunted aspect of the trees and shrubs, and the lazy, careless air of the few French traders and the half-breeds lounging about the wharves. In almost every direction may be seen encampments of Indians; a large body of the Chippewas whose lands were ceded several years ago, continuing to live here. The only link between them and civilization is their propensity to bargaining, and arraying themselves in such fantastic finery as they can afford to purchase, which forms, with their paint and feathers, a ludicrous mixture of costumes. The warriors go armed with tomahawks and scalping knives, but seem entirely peaceable when not infuriated with liquor. They had little reason to be pleased with our coming, the object having been to remove them to Fond du Lac by order of government. The chiefs held a council, and manifested such unwillingness to go that no effort was made to compel them. Some of the braves rewarded our complaisance with the privilege of hearing their songs and whoops and seeing a war-dance around a pole from which streamed the flag of the Union. Several offered their bows and arrows, pipes, etc. for sale, and one who wore a cap made of a heron skin, the feathers of the tail and wings fashioned into a plume that waved with every breeze, touched it with the significant "how schwap?" which seemed to be all they understood of English. I could not prevail on another to part with his bear's claw necklace, even by large offers.

We had arrived very early in the morning, and had an opportunity of observing their manner of lodging, by peeping into several of the wigwams. These are of different fashion from those of the Sioux, both ends of a long pole being driven into the ground, forming a rounded frame, and this covered with strips of birch bark. The fire is built in the centre, the smoke escaping through a hole in the roof, and around it a dozen or more, young and old, male and female, were lying on mats or blankets, with their feet to the fire. In one I saw a Frenchman, lying a little apart from the rest, and in another a medicine man chanting a prayer over a sick child, accompanying it with the monotonous beat of a drum.

A story was here related by a person who had spent much time among the Ojibwas, which illustrates some of their customs. Ondaig (the Crow), the son of one of their most powerful chiefs, was brave and generous, and had distinguished himself in the chase, and in several excursions against the Sioux. He had taken up his winter abode, with his wife and little son, at some distance from his band, according to the custom when game was scarce; and one morning started for a deer hunt after a light fall of snow. His wife thought little of his not returning at night, but when the third day passed, she left her boy in the lodge with the dog for his companion, and set off in search of her husband. Following his track in the snow, till night, she found his blanket on a stick, by which she knew something must have happened. Dreading to meet the fatal knowledge, and anxious for her child, she retraced her steps, and pursuing her journey through the night, reached the wigwam the next morning. She then sought aid from her nearest neighbor, and with her friends again set off to seek the hunter. They encamped where they found the blanket, and on the following morning discovered Ondaig's body leaning against a tree, and stiffened in death, his favorite dog crouched at his feet, and almost exhausted with hunger. The branch of a tree must have struck him in falling, for his skull was fractured; he had probably cut down the tree to capture some animal, and had retained consciousness for a few moments after the blow; for the tracks in the snow showed that he had walked several times round the tree; and his gun, and the bag containing his tobacco and ammunition, were beside him.

There was lamentation in the village when the Indians returned with the remains of the brave Ondaig. To have fallen in battle, or perished by tortures in the midst of enemies would have been a glorious death; but it was hard to die alone in the wilderness like a wild beast. The funeral of the young chief—which the narrator attended, was performed with the ceremonies due a warrior of repute. The faithful dog that had been the only witness of his death, was killed and laid beside him, with his war and hunting implements; his pipe, tobacco and some provisions being placed at his feet. A great feast was prepared, the meat consisting of dog's flesh, the relatives of the deceased, and the chiefs and warriors of his tribe, conducting the ceremonies in profound silence, dressed in their war costumes, with their faces blackened. The nearest relatives were clad in rags, painted black, and had their hair dishevelled. After the feast, and incantations recited by one of their priests, the body was borne to the grave, those who accompanied it dancing and singing a wild chant, and dancing around the grave for half an hour after the dead was laid in it. Another solemn feast was then held at the lodge of Ondaig's aged father. Daily offerings of tobacco, sugar, and other luxuries, were laid on the mound raised over the grave, by the mourning friends, and frequently a group might be seen seated there, smoking and feasting, while their tears were flowing for the deceased. The widow was doomed to five years servitude among her husband's relations, according to their custom, the length of time being always in proportion to the esteem in which the deceased was held while living, but never exceeding five or six years. All kinds of labor, menial offices, and even blows must be submitted to by the bereaved wife, who is considered the property of the nearest relative. The widow of Ondaig accordingly received the severest treatment in the lodge of her father-in-law (the Buffalo), unkindness and taunts to her being esteemed a proper tribute to the memory of her husband.

XV.

"I WOULD rather," said an intelligent traveller, "have seen the Mammoth Cave than Niagara." Many descriptions of its wonders have been published, yet such is the variety of these that each visitor is tempted to record his own impressions, perhaps with the vain idea that *his* picture may do something of the justice others have failed to render. Without any such hope, and merely with the intent of provoking among my readers curiosity to see for themselves, I offer a mere sketch hastily noted down after a walk through the cave. A fuller description I thought at the time unnecessary, as a lady of our party intended to prepare one for a volume of travels.

"Bell's Hotel"—the proprietor of which, with his snow-white locks, and rough, but kind manners, is a curiosity in himself—is on the stage road from Louisville to Nashville, seven or eight miles from the cave. The road to the cave is irregular, stony and shocking, with abrupt descents and steep ascents, and with horses as refractory as those provided for our party, you may stand a chance (excuse the Hibernianism) to walk most of the way. On the top of the last hill you enter a gate and cross a lawn of smooth verdure, surrounded by a range of cabins, drawing up in front of a respectable, ancient looking hotel, the hive to which belongs this swarm of rustic domicils. Into one of these you are presently conducted. It is built of logs whitewashed, and between the chinks a little sunshine is visible here and there; windows in front and rear furnish a refreshing draught of air; the middle of the floor is covered with a piece of carpet, and a fourpost-bed, a small table, a looking-glass, and a few wooden chairs complete the furniture. Abundance of water and clean coarse towels show, however, that the chief requisite to comfort is not neglected. Having dined, supposing your drive or walk from Bell's to have taken up the greater part of the morning, you are desirous of a visit to the palace of gnomes. A winding path through picturesque woods leads to a little dell, where you see the mouth. It is not very large, but the cold draught of air that meets you as you step down from the first ledge of rocks, and the blank gloom glaring from the abyss within, give one a shuddering sensation at first. The rock is festooned and covered with moss of the richest green, the sides are curtained with foliage, and a small broken ladder resting against the space, overgrown with moss, is a picturesque object. You now descend several feet; the guide is ready, and a lighted lamp is put into the hand of each of the party, with a direction to shade it carefully, that it may not be extinguished by the current of air felt for a few moments after entering. Leaving the daylight you go on by a narrow vaulted passage, passing the "Kentucky Cliffs," till you emerge in "the Rotunda," where the ceiling rises to a considerable height, and the walls recede, forming a large apartment. Several wooden pipes and troughs formerly used in the manufacture of saltpetre, are seen in the cave for the first mile or so. Passing under the "Grand Arch," a lofty avenue, the ceiling of which is smooth as sculptured stone, the "Church" is reached, nearly a mile from the entrance. This is a spacious hall with irregular rocky sides, which derives its name from a ledge of rocks resembling a pulpit, forty or fifty feet in height. Sermons have been preached in this place, and I know not where words of solemn import could be so impressively uttered. The visitor finds little fatigue, unless previously exhausted in walking; for there is a peculiar quality in the atmosphere, which invigorates the whole frame, and renders the step light and buoyant. It is said that nothing will decay within the cave, and meat is preserved for weeks by being placed near the entrance. The temperature of the atmosphere never varies during the year, and on this account it has proved beneficial to persons afflicted with pulmonary complaints. Beyond the Church are low stone houses, with floored apartments in which invalids have resided for months. At one time there was quite a street of those dwellings, the inmates of which, it is said, were very sociable and merry in their exclusion from daylight; but most of the habitations have been pulled down. The proprietor of the grounds found it necessary to prevent the thronging of sick persons to the cave, as many of them, beyond cure, died and were buried in the vicinity.

After passing the Church, the gypsum formations begin to assume a singular character, resembling streaks of snow on a dark ground. The ceiling is very lofty, and the avenues wide, conducting to a weird region, like Rübezahl's Hall. Presently we enter the "Star-Chamber." This is, in my opinion, the most wonderful of all the marvels of the cave. You seem to stand in the bottom of a narrow, deep ravine, and look up to the vault of a dark sky.

On either side far up—the rugged steep
Towering like giant cliffs of some deep rift
Cleft in the mountain's breast; upon its crest
A crown of snow, touched by the moon's pale beam;
Above, an arch like midnight's hyaline,
Studded with myriad stars! The fleecy clouds
Like flakes of silver lie beneath; all still,
For no breeze gives them motion; and the stars
Gleam in quick scintillations, till it seems
The solid roof is cleft, and on our gaze
Heaven's own bright lamps are burning! There the Dove
Spreads her soft pinions; there the Pleiades
Shine on their silver throne; with keener eye
Looks forth Orion, and the radiant Ship
That round the firmament hung like a sea
From immemorial time has sailed!

The grand proportions of this place, and the height of the mysterious firmament, favor the illusion, which is so perfect that it is difficult to persuade yourself you are not gazing upon the midnight heaven. A fine effect is produced by the removal of the lights to a distant point among the rocks.

The "Gothic Avenue" is reached by ascending a flight of steps on the right, after passing the Church;

it is lofty and spacious. Beyond is the "Haunted Chamber," a more humble apartment, so called from the fact that Indian mummies were found in one of its recesses. It is easy to imagine that the cave might have been used as a place of sepulture by an aboriginal race; though bodies have never been found in any other part of it. The next place of note is the "Gothic Chapel," a vast chamber, interspersed with stalactites of a dark color, resembling gothic pillars wreathed with elaborate ornaments, with richly fretted ceiling and walls, and an altar of curious workmanship, incrusted with tangled masses of ornamental carving. The guide took our lamps, and hung them upon different pillars, greatly heightening the effect, and giving the chapel the appearance of being lighted up for a midnight funeral ceremony. The visitor who admires the sublime in picturesque scenery, will linger long in this solemn and strangely beautiful sanctuary of nature. There is but one thing to mar the effect, and that is, the number of names smoked on the ceiling. Through all parts of the cave which are usually visited, this hateful practice has defaced the walls.

Beyond the chapel is a curious intertwining of formations called the "Devil's Arm Chair,"—Ammett's Dome, etc. But few go farther in this branch. The route usually taken by those who wish to explore is a different one, and requires the devotion of an entire day; so that you will be kind enough, in imagination, to retrace your steps, and return to the open air; pausing to observe, as the first gleam of daylight greets the vision, how beautifully it flashes across "the raven down of darkness."

On the following morning, after a very early breakfast, the ladies arrayed themselves in costume resembling the "Bloomer," as picturesque as red or blue flannel could make it, and commenced the pilgrimage anew. Not far from the Church is a curious fragment of rock called the "Giant's Coffin," from its shape; behind this is a narrow, descending pathway, over which the rocks project so as to render stooping necessary; this leads to the subterranean river. This labyrinthine way enters the "Deserted Chamber." "Fat Man's Misery" is a winding passage between rocky walls, distressing to such worthies as emulate Daniel Lambert. "The Bacon Room" is thickly hung with stalactites of a uniform size, resembling hams incased in whitewashed coverings. I cannot pretend to give the names of all the halls, avenues, apartments, pits, etc., we passed; such an enumeration would be tedious, as many of the places are named merely for the convenience of designation, or to determine distances. Sometimes we entered a chamber from which there seemed no possible egress, till, on ascending a heap of rocks, an opening appeared in the ceiling, with a ladder; or a similar one in the floor disclosed a flight of steps; or some unexpected turn showed a narrow opening, concealed by projecting rocks, which conducted to spacious halls, where new marvels were seen. These openings were presented continually; sometimes so small as hardly to admit the body, and all leading to avenues and branches of the cave. The number of these branches, and the complexity of the labyrinthine passages, render it dangerous for any visitor, unattended by a guide, to attempt an exploration.

The voice of the guide is heard about this time, warning against the pits that threaten to swallow up the unwary traveller; the largest of these, however, are sufficiently fenced for the purpose of security. "Side-saddle Pit" is the first deep one; a fragment of burning paper thrown down, or a Bengal light, discloses a fearful abyss, not much wider than a well. The "Bottomless Pit," further on, across the wooden bridge, is yet more appalling. Leaning over the frail fence, you peer into a fathomless profundity of gloom, the uttermost spaces of which cannot be seen even by the glaring lustre of the torch. Stones thrown down rattle against the sides, but are not heard to touch the bottom; being probably buried in the mud. The guide informed us he had frequently been let down in a basket.

Many objects of curiosity were passed, each worthy of a particular description. One large fragment of rock is called the "Great Western," from its resemblance to a ship. "Martha's Vineyard" is reached by climbing a tall ladder; the formations, in size, shape and color, are like rich clusters of grapes, a winding crevice in the roof serving for the vine. On the side of this place appears an opening above a precipitous wall, reached by clambering from ledge to ledge; it leads, Stephen informed us, to "Purgatory," so called because it was "a tight place to get through;" a passage visitors sometimes take to the river. Another wonder of the cave, not now visited on account of the difficulty of access, is a small chamber above, called the "Holy Sepulchre," where is a rock shaped exactly like a tomb. Above this is suspended a single immense stalactite, which, when struck, gave a sound like the tolling of a bell, till injured by a sacrilegious visitor, who broke off a piece. In the ledges of these rocks are cool, gushing springs, some of which fling down their tributes in miniature cascades. There are said to be several cataracts in the cave, but we could not obtain a sight of any.

After passing "the black hole of Calcutta,"—an unguarded pit—an abyss on one side roofed with rock, through the rifts in which stones fall plashing into water, is the "Dead Sea." It is the beginning of the river, which further on is called "Styx," and is crossed on an arch of rocks termed the "Natural Bridge." The walking in many places hereabouts is slippery and difficult. "Lake Lethe," the first portion of the river on which the traveller embarks, in the small flat boat moored at its side, is a dark, sullen stream, walled in by precipitous rocks, and is said to be of considerable depth. Fish are caught in these waters of small size, white, and destitute of eyes, which are preserved in alcohol, and sold as curiosities. The only other living creature except crickets, found is a kind of rat, also white, bearing some resemblance to a squirrel. Not a shred of vegetation is seen.

The next portion of water scenery is called "Echo River"—and well it is named; for strains of more dulcet melody and deliciously plaintive cadences were never called forth by the Nightingale herself, than float through these rocky recesses in answer to notes of music. The plash of the oar sounded like the gibbering of spirit voices. The massive roof bends at intervals to within a few feet of the dark waters, which wind their way picturesquely between the cliffs.

> There is a place, where viewless spirits of sound
> Their birth-place have, deep hidden from the day;
> Where solid mountains piled, o'erarch the dome,
> And rivers wander, hemmed by bending rocks,
> In the embrace of everlasting night;
> And there the inner harmonies of earth
> Sleep in their caves; or, waked too suddenly,
> Utter their 'plaint in murmurs quick and soft,
> Dying in faintest cadence, till again
> Old silence drinks the tones; or roused to glee,
> Fill all the air with dancing melodies;
> Fling sportive whisperings to the sullen wave
> With sweet unearthly voices,—each wild note
> By myriads answered in receding music,
> Till mortal sense, bewildered, seems to hear
> The echo of the distant harps of heaven.

Some three miles of rough and tedious walking over broken and jagged rocks bring you to the most beautiful parts of the cave. "Cleveland's Cabinet" is a museum of wonders. Fancy apartments thickly encrusted with small glistening stalactites, flowers, leaves, and wreaths of snowy whiteness, walls and ceiling converted into a luxuriant arbor, where the mimic foliage is interspersed with fruits and pendent gems, all in such dazzling profusion that it mocks the wealth of Flora. It is like the most exquisite waxwork, and executed with a delicacy and richness no art could equal. Roses, lilies, and garlands of flowers wrought like nature, and more elaborate than ever adorned Corinthian capital, decorate this wondrous temple. The scientific visitor might spend months in the examination of this delicate tracery, and find something new to delight him.

"Snowball Room" is incrusted with lime formations resembling sparkling snowballs, thickly planted on the ceiling and sides. "Diamond Hall" is dazzling with the incrustations of mimic gems, that flash back the light like jewels of Golconda. Leaving these beautiful lime formations, you proceed, having paid no attention to the avenue leading to "the grotto of Egeria," for time presses, and the way is yet far. Passing other halls, and an interminable avenue, "the Rocky Mountains" rise as barriers to further progress. These are formed by rocks fallen from the top of the cave, and are said to be one hundred feet in height. The steep and rough ascent must be climbed by the adventurous wanderer; for nature remits not her penalties for any who venture so far into her weird sanctuary. Having reached the top, a glance to the right shows a broken space, filled with thick and heavy darkness; and presently a crimson light on the farther side at one or two points, throws a fitful illumination on the "Dismal Hollow,"—a place that seems the chosen retreat of the gnomes that range in the central regions of the earth. It calls to mind all the tales of genii, and wild subterranean haunts of robbers that beguiled our childhood, till the imagination kindles with the strange romance of the scene. A steep but easy descent conducts to "Serena's Harbor," the termination of this branch of the cave. Here a grove of stalactites of a yellowish color, with arched roof and smooth floor, offers a pleasant resting place. Nine miles have been traversed from the entrance, and you wish to be lifted to upper air through some chasm in the roof. No such friendly rift, however, appears, and your only resource is to retrace your steps through the crystal chambers, and across the mysterious rivers. You find the daylight fading from the sky as you emerge from the cave; or if you have done justice to its beauties, the night will be far advanced towards another dawn.

"Goram's Dome" is usually spoken of as the greatest curiosity in the cave, and is in its deepest part. The path leading to it turns off to the right from the Bottomless Pit; and after descending ladders and flights of steps, sometimes winding along the verge of rocky dells, and treading low winding passages, you stand before an opening in the solid rock, resembling a Gothic window. Looking through this, you see a chamber four or five hundred feet in height, the arched dome of which, seen when illuminated, is regular and smooth as sculptured marble, as are the sides of its profound depths, to the bottom of which the eye cannot reach. The peculiar feature of the apartment is a partition wall, resembling a vast curtain, the carved cornices and architraves of which mock the triumphs of art. The water trickling down the folds of this massive drapery alone breaks the solemn silence. Some thirty feet down, the wall is abruptly cut off, and overhangs the well below. It will be long before the gazer can turn away from a sight so full of grandeur.

Many other places remained unvisited on account of the brief time at our disposal. "Bats' Chamber," where myriads of these creatures cling to the wall motionless, is near the entrance. "Lake Purity" is a small sheet at the foot of a hill of rocks, and several more were described by visitors who had been able to spend weeks in the vicinity. We were obliged to content ourselves with the knowledge that we had seen more than the majority. The cave is said to contain two hundred and twenty-six avenues, and forty-seven domes. The walking is generally dry, and not dangerous if the directions of the guide are followed. No one should venture without such a companion, for he would be almost certain to lose his way among the intricate passages. Accidents sometimes happen under the best auspices. We found the oil exhausted at one of the oil stations, and were obliged to extinguish some of our lamps to provide against an emergency. A young gentleman who was spending the beginning of his honeymoon at the cave, came near meeting with serious inconvenience from a piece of negligence of this sort. He was going alone to the end with the guide, who left him for half an hour to make an excursion. During his absence, desirous of experiencing the effect of total darkness, he extinguished his lamp. As they were walking on, the guide's lamp suddenly went out; his own, having a small remnant of oil, continued to burn, though more and more dimly. Their walk was now quickened to a run, and by good luck they had arrived within sight of the next oil station, when they were immersed in utter darkness. Had it not been for the fortunate accident of extinguishing his lamp, they would have been compelled to remain, seven miles from the entrance, until missed and sent for from the hotel, for not the most experienced guide could grope his way safely more than a few yards.

"White's Cave" is about three quarters of a mile distant, and is described as filled with formations of remarkable beauty. The whole country, indeed, abounds in subterranean chambers, being a perfect *honeycomb*, it is said, beneath the surface of the earth.

THE END.

www.ingramcontent.com/pod-product-compliance
Lightning Source LLC
LaVergne TN
LVHW010232110826
845151LV00004B/1268
* 9 7 8 1 4 2 5 5 2 4 8 0 7 *